T0019382

CONTENTS

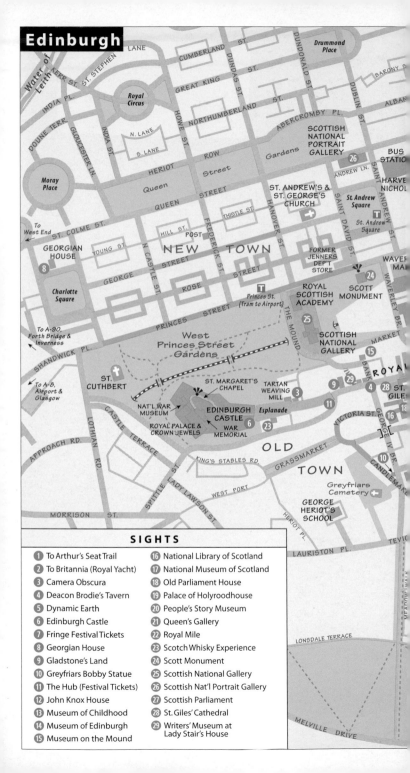

Edinburgh

SIGHTS

1. To Arthur's Seat Trail
2. To Britannia (Royal Yacht)
3. Camera Obscura
4. Deacon Brodie's Tavern
5. Dynamic Earth
6. Edinburgh Castle
7. Fringe Festival Tickets
8. Georgian House
9. Gladstone's Land
10. Greyfriars Bobby Statue
11. The Hub (Festival Tickets)
12. John Knox House
13. Museum of Childhood
14. Museum of Edinburgh
15. Museum on the Mound
16. National Library of Scotland
17. National Museum of Scotland
18. Old Parliament House
19. Palace of Holyroodhouse
20. People's Story Museum
21. Queen's Gallery
22. Royal Mile
23. Scotch Whisky Experience
24. Scott Monument
25. Scottish National Gallery
26. Scottish Nat'l Portrait Gallery
27. Scottish Parliament
28. St. Giles' Cathedral
29. Writers' Museum at Lady Stair's House

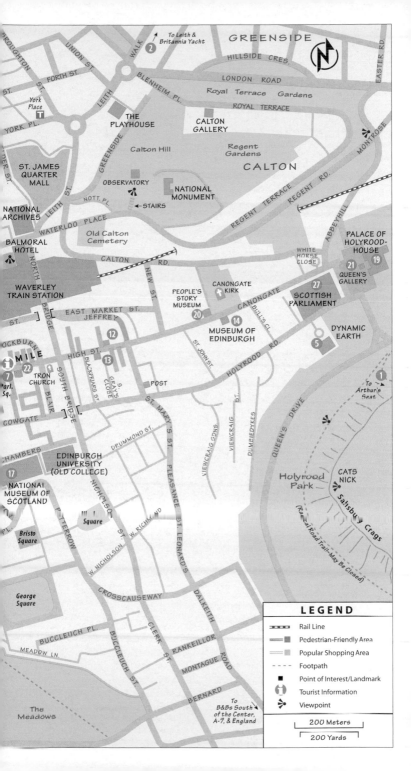

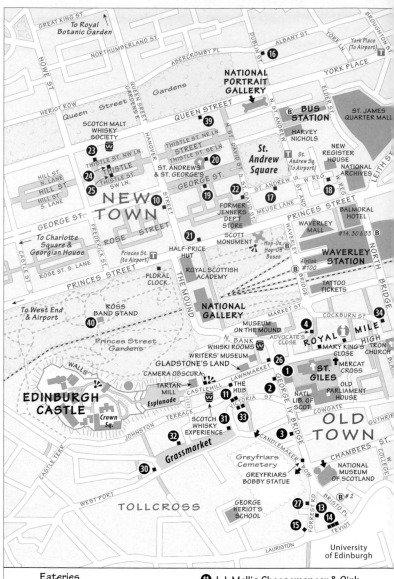

Eateries

1. Le Bistrot
2. Ondine Seafood Restaurant
3. The Outsider
4. Devil's Advocate
5. Wedgwood Restaurant
6. David Bann Vegetarian Rest.
7. Edinburgh Larder
8. Mimi's Little Bakehouse
9. Clarinda's Tea Room
10. Oink (2)
11. I.J. Mellis Cheesemonger & Oink
12. The Haggis Box
13. Union of Genius & Mums
14. Ting Thai Caravan, Saboteur & El Cartel
15. Civerinos Slice
16. The Magnum Restaurant & Bar
17. Dishoom
18. Café Royal
19. The Dome Restaurant
20. St. Andrew's & St. George's Church Undercroft Café

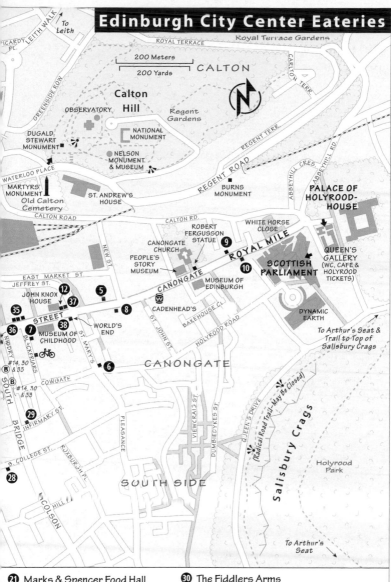

Edinburgh City Center Eateries

200 Meters
200 Yards

CALTON

Royal Terrace Gardens
ROYAL TERRACE
PICARDY PL.
LEITH WALK
To Leith

Calton Hill

OBSERVATORY

Regent Gardens

GREENSIDE ROW

N

DUGALD STEWART MUNUMENT

NATIONAL MONUMENT

NELSON MONUMENT & MUSEUM

REGENT TERR.

CARLTON TERR.

ABBEYHILL CRES

ABBEYHILL RD.

WATERLOO PLACE

MARTYRS' MONUMENT

Old Calton Cemetery

ST. ANDREW'S HOUSE

REGENT ROAD

BURNS MONUMENT

CALTON ROAD

CALTON RD.

PALACE OF HOLYROOD-HOUSE

WHITE HORSE CLOSE

EAST MARKET ST.

NEW ST.

JEFFREY ST.

ROBERT FERGUSSON STATUE

CANONGATE CHURCH

PEOPLE'S STORY MUSEUM

CANONGATE

MUSEUM OF EDINBURGH

ROYAL MILE

❾

❿

SCOTTISH PARLIAMENT

QUEEN'S GALLERY (WC, CAFE & HOLYROOD TICKETS)

❶❷

JOHN KNOX HOUSE

❺

❸❼

CADENHEAD'S

BAKEHOUSE CL.

DYNAMIC EARTH

❸❺

STREET

❽

❸❻

❼

MUSEUM OF CHILDHOOD

❸❽

WORLD'S END

HOLYROOD ROAD

To Arthur's Seat & Trail to Top of Salisbury Crags

BLACKFRIARS

ST. MARY'S

ST. JOHN ST.

B #14, 30 & 35

B #14, 30 & 35

COWGATE

❻

CANONGATE

SOUTH BRIDGE

❷❾

INFIRMARY ST.

PLEASANCE

VIEWCRAIG ST.

DUMBIEDYKES ST.

QUEEN'S DRIVE (Radical Road Trail—May Be Closed)

Salisbury Crags

Holyrood Park

S. COLLEGE ST.

ROXBURGH PL.

ROXBURGH ST.

HILL PL.

COLSON

SOUTH SIDE

❷❽

To Arthur's Seat

---

❷❶ Marks & Spencer Food Hall
❷❷ Sainsbury's
❷❸ Le Café St. Honoré
❷❹ The Bon Vivant
❷❺ Fishers in the City

Pubs & Nightlife
❷❻ Deacon Brodie's Tavern
❷❼ Sandy Bell's Pub
❷❽ Captain's Bar
❷❾ The Royal Oak Pub

❸⓪ The Fiddlers Arms
❸❶ Biddy Mulligans
❸❷ White Hart Inn
❸❸ Finnegans Wake & The Bow Bar
❸❹ The Scotsman's Lounge
❸❺ Whiski Bar, Royal Mile, Mitre Bar
❸❻ Whistle Binkies Bar
❸❼ No. 1 High Street Pub
❸❽ The World's End Pub
❸❾ Spirit of Scotland Show
❹⓪ Princes Street Gardens Dancers

INTRODUCTION

This Snapshot guide, excerpted from my guidebook *Rick Steves Scotland*, introduces you to the rugged, feisty, colorful capital city of Edinburgh. A hubbub of innovation and tradition, this urbane city rambles along seven hills on the banks of the Firth of Forth. Its historic Royal Mile links Edinburgh Castle—home of Mary Queen of Scots—to the Palace of Holyroodhouse, the home away from home of King Charles III. To the north is the city's New Town, a characteristic 18th-century neighborhood of Georgian mansions and upscale hangouts.

Edinburgh is the political, cultural, and intellectual center of Scotland, but intrepid visitors can still find a few surviving rough edges of "Auld Reekie," as it was once called (for the smell of smoke during the Victorian era). Take a walk along historic cobbled streets and narrow lanes, tracing the footsteps of Robert Burns and Robert Louis Stevenson. Sip whisky with an expert and see firsthand how Scotland's national drink can become, as they're fond of saying, "a very good friend." Debate the pros and cons of Scottish independence on the steps of the 21st-century parliament building. Through it all, be prepared for a Scottish charm offensive that will make you want to stay longer in one of Europe's most intoxicating capitals.

To help you have the best trip possible, I've included the following topics in this book:

• **Planning Your Time,** with advice on how to make the most of your limited time

• **Orientation,** including tourist information (abbreviated as TI), tips on public transportation, local tour options, and helpful hints

• **Sights,** with ratings and strategies for meaningful and efficient visits

• **Sleeping** and **Eating,** with good-value recommendations in every price range

• **Connections,** with tips on trains, buses, and driving

Practicalities, near the end of this book, has information on money, staying connected, hotel reservations, transportation, and other helpful hints.

To travel smartly, read this little book in its entirety before you go. It's my hope that this guide will make your trip more meaningful and rewarding. Traveling like a temporary local, you'll get the absolute most out of every mile, minute, and dollar.

Happy travels!

Rick Steves

EDINBURGH

Edinburgh is the historical, cultural, and political capital of Scotland. For nearly a thousand years, Scotland's kings, parliaments, writers, thinkers, and bankers have called Edinburgh home. Today, it remains Scotland's most sophisticated city.

Edinburgh (ED'n-burah—only tourists pronounce it like "Pittsburgh") is Scotland's showpiece and one of Europe's most entertaining cities. It's a place of stunning vistas—nestled among craggy bluffs and studded with a prickly skyline of spires, towers, domes, and steeples. Proud statues of famous Scots dot the urban landscape. The buildings are a harmonious yellow-gray, all built from the same local sandstone.

Culturally, Edinburgh has always been the place where Lowland culture (urban and English) met Highland style (rustic and Gaelic). Tourists will find no end of traditional Scottish clichés. whisky tastings, kilt shops, bagpipe-playing buskers, and gimmicky tours featuring Scotland's bloody history and ghost stories.

Edinburgh is two cities in one. The Old Town stretches along the Royal Mile, from the grand castle on top to the palace on the bottom. Along this colorful labyrinth of cobbled streets and narrow lanes, medieval skyscrapers stand shoulder to shoulder, hiding peaceful courtyards.

A few hundred yards north of the Old Town lies the New Town. It's a magnificent planned neighborhood (from the 1700s). Here, you'll enjoy upscale shops, broad boulevards, straight streets, square squares, circular circuses, and Georgian mansions decked out in Greek-style columns and statues.

Just to the west of the New Town, the West End is a prestigious and quieter neighborhood boasting more Georgian architecture, cobbled lanes, fine dining options, and a variety of concert and theater venues.

Today's Edinburgh is big in banking, scientific research, and scholarship at its four universities. Since 1999, when Scotland regained a measure of self-rule, Edinburgh reassumed its place as home of the Scottish Parliament. The city hums with life. Students and professionals pack the pubs and art galleries. It's especially lively in August, when the Edinburgh Festival takes over the town. Historic, monumental, fun, and well organized, Edinburgh is a tourist's delight.

PLANNING YOUR TIME

While the major sights can be seen in a day, I'd give Edinburgh two days and three nights.

Day 1: Tour the castle, then take my self-guided Royal Mile walk, stopping in at St. Giles' Cathedral and whichever shops and museums interest you (Gladstone's Land is especially worthwhile). At the bottom of the Mile, consider visiting the Scottish Parliament, the Palace of Holyroodhouse, or both. If the weather's good (and the trail is open), you could hike back to your B&B below Arthur's Seat.

Day 2: Visit the National Museum of Scotland. After lunch, stroll through the Scottish National Gallery. Then follow my self-guided walk through the New Town, visiting the Scottish National Portrait Gallery and the Georgian House—or zip out to Leith to squeeze in a quick tour of the good ship *Britannia* (confirm last entry time before you go).

Evenings: Options include various "haunted Edinburgh" walks, the literary pub crawl, or live music in pubs. Sadly, full-blown traditional folk performances are just about extinct, surviving only in excruciatingly schmaltzy variety shows put on for tour-bus groups. Perhaps the most authentic evening out is just settling down in a pub to sample the whisky and local beers while meeting the locals...and attempting to understand them through their thick Scottish accents.

Orientation to Edinburgh

A VERBAL MAP

With 500,000 people (835,000 in the metro area), Edinburgh is Scotland's second-biggest city, after Glasgow. But the tourist's Edinburgh is compact: Old Town, New Town, West End, and the B&B area south of the city center.

Edinburgh's **Old Town** stretches across a ridgeline slung between two bluffs. From west to east, this "Royal Mile" runs from the Castle Rock—which is visible from anywhere in town—to

EDINBURGH

the base of the 822-foot extinct volcano called Arthur's Seat. For visitors, this east-west axis is the center of the action. Just south of the Royal Mile are the university and the National Museum of Scotland; farther to the south is a handy B&B neighborhood that lines up along **Dalkeith Road** and **Mayfield Gardens.** North of the Royal Mile ridge is the **New Town,** a neighborhood of grid-planned streets and elegant Georgian buildings, and the **West End,** near Charlotte Square—a posh, quiet neighborhood that's still close to the sightseeing action.

In the center of it all—in a drained lakebed between the Old and New Towns—sit the Princes Street Gardens park and Waverley Bridge, where you'll find Waverley train station, Waverley Mall, a bus info office (starting point for most city bus tours), the Scottish National Gallery, and a covered dance-and-music pavilion.

TOURIST INFORMATION

The TI, branded "iCentre," is on the Royal Mile across from St. Giles' Cathedral. Though the office has the feel of a booking agency for local tours, the laptop-equipped staff can answer most questions (Mon-Sat 9:30-17:30, Sun 10:00-17:00; July-Aug Mon-Sat 9:30-19:00, Sun 10:00-18:00; 249 High Street, +44 131 473 3820, www.visitscotland.com).

For more information than what's included in the TI's free map, buy the excellent *Collins Discovering Edinburgh* map (which comes with opinionated commentary and locates almost every major sight). If you're interested in evening music, ask for the free monthly *Gig Guide*.

Sightseeing Passes: Edinburgh Tours sells a £63 **Royal Edinburgh Ticket** that covers 48 hours of unlimited travel on three different hop-on, hop-off buses (described under "Tours in Edinburgh," later), plus admission at Edinburgh Castle, the Palace of Holyroodhouse, and the Royal Yacht *Britannia* (www. royaledinburghticket.co.uk). This is a good deal if you plan to use the buses and see all three sights. If your travels take you beyond Edinburgh, consider the **Historic Scotland's Explorer Pass,** which can save money if you visit the castles at both Edinburgh and Stirling, or are also visiting the Orkney Islands (for details, see www.historicenvironment.scot). You'll need to book an entry time for Edinburgh Castle with either pass.

EDINBURGH

ARRIVAL IN EDINBURGH

By Train: Most long-distance trains arrive at **Waverley Station** in the city center (those staying at one of my recommended West End accommodations might consider disembarking instead at **Haymarket Station**). For more specifics on linking to my recommended hotel neighborhoods, see the "Sleeping in Edinburgh" section, later. Waverley Station is a bit of a maze; follow signs carefully to find your way. For groceries to go, M&S Simply Food, near track 2, is economical and efficient (long hours daily). There are three major exits:

Princes Street Exit: Use this exit to reach **buses** to B&Bs south of the city center. Follow signs for *#1, Princes Street.* You'll ride a series of escalators (passing the Waverley Mall on your left) and pop out along busy Princes Street, facing the New Town. Turn right along Princes Street, then right again along North Bridge, and look for the stop for buses #14, #30, and #33.

Waverley Bridge Exit: This exit sends you up a long ramp; you'll pop out between the Old Town and the New Town, handy for those who'd like to **walk** to either area.

Market Street Exit: The nearest official **taxi** stand is outside the Market Street exit. Once outside, turn left and walk 100 yards under the bridge to find the taxis.

By Bus: Scottish Citylink, Megabus, and National Express buses use the bus station (with luggage lockers) in the New Town, two blocks north of Waverley Station on St. Andrew Square.

By Car: No matter where you're coming from, avoid needless driving in the city by taking advantage of Edinburgh's bypass road, A-720. To conveniently reach my recommended B&Bs, circle the city on the A-720 (direction: Edinburgh South), until the last roundabout, named *Sheriffhall*. Exit the roundabout at the first left *(A-7 Edinburgh)*. From here it's four miles to the B&B neighborhood south of the center. After a while, the A-7 becomes Dalkeith Road. If you see the huge Royal Commonwealth Pool, you've gone a couple of blocks too far.

By Plane: Edinburgh's airport is eight miles west of downtown—about a 30-minute tram or taxi ride. For information, see "Edinburgh Connections," at the end of this chapter.

HELPFUL HINTS

Markets: On weekends, open-air markets have food stalls and artisans (10:00 16:00, www.stockbridgemarket.com). Saturday is at Grassmarket (below the castle) and in Leith (at Dock Place), plus there's a Saturday morning farmers market in the Edinburgh Castle parking lot. Sunday is market day in Stockbridge along Saunders Street and the Water of Leith Walkway.

Festivals: August is a crowded, popular month to visit Edinburgh thanks to the multiple festivals hosted here, including the official Edinburgh International Festival, the Fringe Festival, and the Military Tattoo. Book ahead for hotels, events, and restaurant dinners, and expect to pay significantly more for your room. Many museums and shops have extended hours in August. For more festival details, see RickSteves.com/festivals.

Baggage Storage: There's a luggage storage office at the train station and cheaper lockers at the bus station on St. Andrew Square, just two blocks north.

Laundry: The **Ace Cleaning Centre** launderette is located between my recommended B&Bs south of town and the city center. You can pay for full-service laundry (drop off in the morning for same-day service) or stay and do it yourself. For

EDINBURGH

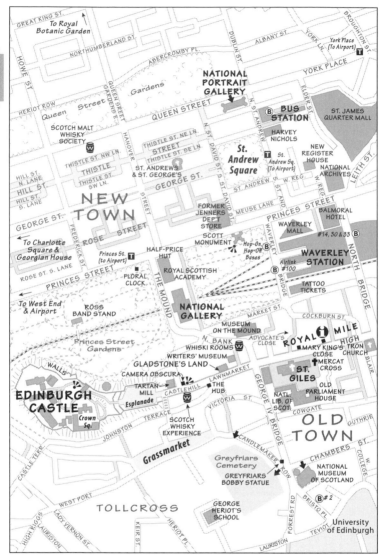

a small extra fee, they may be willing to collect your laundry from your B&B and/or drop it off the next day (Mon-Fri 8:00-19:30, Sat 9:00-17:00, Sun 10:00-16:00, right at the Bernard Terrace bus stop along bus route to city center, 13 South Clerk Street—see map on page 104, +44 131 667 0549, www.acelaunderetteanddrycleaners.co.uk). In the West End, **Johnsons the Cleaners** will do your laundry (no hotel or B&B drop-off, Mon-Fri 8:30-17:30, Sat until 17:00, closed Sun, 5 Drumsheugh Place—see map on page 101, +44 131 225 8077).

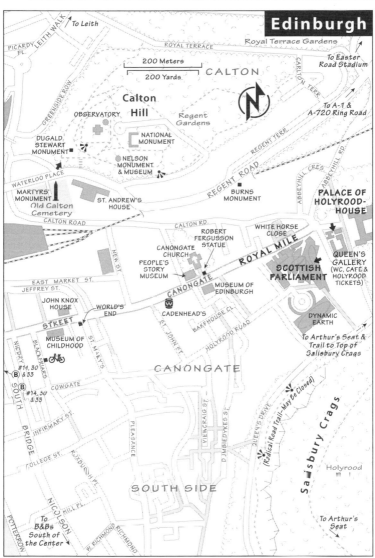

Bike Rental and Tours: The laid-back crew at **Cycle Scotland** happily recommends good bike routes with your rental (£30/day, e-bikes available, generally open daily 10:00-18:00, may close off-season, just off Royal Mile at 29 Blackfriars Street, +44 131 556 5560, mobile +44 779 688 6899, www.cyclescotland. co.uk, Peter). They also run guided three-hour bike tours daily at 11:00 (and sometimes at 15:00) that start on the Royal Mile and ride through Holyrood Park, Arthur's Seat, Duddingston Village, Doctor Neil's (Secret) Garden, and along the Innocent railway path (£50/person, £70/person for e-bikes, book ahead).

Car Rental: These places have offices both in Edinburgh and at the airport: **Avis** (24 East London Street, +44 344 544 6059, airport +44 344 544 9064), **Europcar** (farther out—on Salamander Road in Leith, +44 371 384 3811, airport +44 371 384 3406), **Hertz** (10 Picardy Place, +44 843 309 3026, airport +44 843 309 3025), and **Budget** (24 East London Street, +44 344 544 9064, airport +44 344 544 4605). Some downtown offices close or have reduced hours on Sunday, but the airport locations tend to be open daily. If you plan to rent a car, pick it up on your way out of Edinburgh—you won't need it in town.

Dress for the Weather: Weather blows in and out—bring your sweater and be prepared for rain.

GETTING AROUND EDINBURGH

By Bus: Many of Edinburgh's sights are within walking distance of one another, but buses come in handy—especially if you're staying at a B&B south of the city center. Double-decker buses come with fine views upstairs.

A single ride costs £1.80; pay with a contactless card or payment app, or with exact change (tell the driver "single ticket"). An all-day ticket costs £4.50 (contactless payment is automatically capped at £4.40/day or £20/week).

Mapping apps like Google Maps work great for determining the best bus for your journey, including real-time departure times and delays. Electronic signs at some stops count down the minutes until the next bus. Pick up a route map at the TI or at the transit office at the Old Town end of Waverley Bridge (+44 131 555 6363, www.lothianbuses.com).

By Tram: Edinburgh's single tram line (£1.80/ride, buy at ticket machine before boarding, credit card or exact change) is designed more for locals than tourists. It's most useful for reaching the airport (£6.50 one-way; see "Edinburgh Connections" at the end of this chapter) or getting from my recommended West End hotels to Princes Street and St. Andrew Square, near the Waverley train station.

By Taxi or Uber: The 1,300 taxis cruising Edinburgh's streets are easy to flag down (a ride between downtown and the B&B neighborhood south of the center costs about £8-10; rates go up after 18:00 and on weekends). Taxis can turn on a dime, so hail them in either direction. You can also use the Free Now app to summon a taxi (easy to set up, works like Uber). Uber works well here and may saves a few pounds (or cost more during "surge" times; use the Free Now app to compare Uber and taxi prices).

Tours in Edinburgh

Royal Mile Walking Tours

Walking tours are an Edinburgh specialty; you'll see groups trailing entertaining guides all over town. Below I've listed good all-purpose walks; for **literary pub crawls** and **ghost tours,** see "Nightlife in Edinburgh" on page 92.

Edinburgh Tour Guides offers a good historical walk (without all the ghosts and goblins). Their Royal Mile tour is a gentle three-hour downhill stroll from the top of the Mile to the palace (£25; daily at 9:30 and 19:00—evening tour is only two hours; meet outside The Hub, near the top of the Royal Mile; must reserve ahead, +44 785 888 0072, www.edinburghtourguides.com, info@ edinburghtourguides.com). Their other offerings include *Outlander*-themed Edinburgh walks and day tours.

Mercat Tours offers a "Secrets of the Royal Mile" walk that's more entertaining than intellectual (£20, 1.5 hours; £38 adds optional, 45-minute guided Edinburgh Castle visit that lets you skip the ticket line; daily at 10:00 and 13:00, leaves from Mercat Cross on the Royal Mile, +44 131 225 5445, www.mercattours.com). The guides, who enjoy making a short story long, ignore the big sights and take you behind the scenes with piles of barely historical gossip, bully-pulpit Scottish pride, and fun but forgettable trivia. They also offer other tours, such as ghost walks, tours of 18th-century Blair Underground Vaults on the southern slope of the Royal Mile, whisky tastings, and *Outlander* sights.

Sandemans New Edinburgh runs "free" tours multiple times a day; you won't pay upfront, but the guide will expect a tip (check schedule online, 2.5 hours, meet at 130 High Street, www. neweuropetours.eu).

The **Voluntary Guides Association** offers free two-hour walks during the Edinburgh Festival. You don't need a reservation—just show up (check website for times, generally depart from City Chambers across from St. Giles' Cathedral on the Royal Mile, www.edinburghfestivalguides.org). You can also hire their guides (for a small fee) for private tours outside of festival time.

Blue Badge Local Guides

The following guides charge similar prices and offer half-day and full-day tours: **Jean Blair** (a delightful teacher and guide, walking tours only—no car, £295/day, £190/half-day, +44 798 957 0287, www.travelthroughscotland.com, scotguide7@gmail.com); **Sergio La Spina** (an Argentinean who adopted Edinburgh as his hometown more than 20 years ago, £250/day, £195/half-day, can also do driving tours, +44 131 664 1731, mobile +44 797 330 6579, www.vivaescocia.com, sergiolaspina@aol.com); **Ken Han-**

Edinburgh at a Glance

▲▲▲**Royal Mile** Historic road—good for walking—stretching from the castle down to the palace, lined with museums, pubs, and shops. See page 15.

▲▲▲**Edinburgh Castle** Iconic hilltop fort and royal residence complete with crown jewels, Romanesque chapel, memorial, and fine military museum. **Hours:** Daily 9:30-18:00, Oct-March until 17:00. See page 37.

▲▲**Gladstone's Land** Seventeenth-century Royal Mile merchant's residence. **Hours:** Daily 10:00-15:00. See page 49.

▲▲**St. Giles' Cathedral** Preaching grounds of Scottish Reformer John Knox, with spectacular organ, Neo-Gothic chapel, and distinctive crown spire. **Hours:** Mon-Fri 10:00-18:00, Sat 9:00-17:00, Sun 13:00-17:00. See page 51.

▲▲**Scottish Parliament Building** Striking headquarters for parliament, which returned to Scotland in 1999. **Hours:** Mon-Sat 10:00-17:00, Tue-Thu 9:00-18:30 when parliament is in session (Sept-June), closed Sun year-round. See page 58.

▲▲**Palace of Holyroodhouse** The British monarchy's official residence in Scotland, with lavish rooms, 12th-century abbey, and gallery with rotating exhibits. **Hours:** Daily 9:30-18:00, Nov-March until 16:30, closed during royal visits. See page 59.

▲▲**National Museum of Scotland** Intriguing, well-displayed artifacts from prehistoric times to the 20th century. **Hours:** Daily 10:00-17:00. See page 62.

▲▲**Scottish National Gallery** Choice sampling of European masters and Scotland's finest. **Hours:** Daily 10:00-17:00. See page 67.

▲▲**Scottish National Portrait Gallery** Beautifully displayed Who's Who of Scottish history. **Hours:** Daily 10:00-17:00. See page 72.

▲▲**Georgian House** Intimate peek at upper-crust life in the late 1700s. **Hours:** Daily 10:00-17:00, shorter hours and possibly closed Nov-March. See page 75.

▲▲**Royal Yacht *Britannia*** The late Queen Elizabeth II's former

EDINBURGH

floating palace, with a history of distinguished passengers, a 15-minute trip out of town. **Hours:** Daily 9:30-16:00, Sept-Oct from 10:00, Nov-March until 15:00. See page 76.

▲**Camera Obscura** Five floors of illusions, holograms, and gags, topped with the best view of the Royal Mile. **Hours:** Daily July-Aug 8:00-22:00, off-season 9:00-19:00—but often until later on weekends. See page 48.

▲**Scotch Whisky Experience** Gimmicky but fun and educational introduction to Scotland's most famous beverage. **Hours:** Generally daily 10:00-18:30. See page 49.

▲**Writers' Museum at Lady Stair's House** Aristocrat's house, built in 1622, filled with artifacts from Robert Burns, Robert Louis Stevenson, and Sir Walter Scott. **Hours:** Daily 10:00-17:00. See page 50.

▲**The Real Mary King's Close** Underground street and houses last occupied in the 17th century, viewable by guided tour. **Hours:** Mon-Fri 9:30-17:00, Sat-Sun until 21:00. See page 55.

▲**Museum of Childhood** Five stories of nostalgic fun. **Hours:** Daily 10:00-17:00. See page 55.

▲**John Knox House** Medieval home with exhibits on the life of Scotland's great Protestant reformer. **Hours:** Daily 10:00-18:00. See page 55.

▲**People's Story Museum** Everyday life from the 18th to 20th century. **Hours:** Daily 10:00-17:00. See page 57.

▲**Museum of Edinburgh** Historic mementos, from the original National Covenant inscribed on animal skin to early golf balls. **Hours:** Daily 10:00-17:00. See page 58.

▲**Queen's Gallery** Intimate museum with treasures from the royal art collection. **Hours:** Daily 9:30-18:00, Nov-March until 16:30. See page 61.

▲**Rosslyn Chapel** Small 15th-century church chock-full of intriguing carvings a short drive outside of Edinburgh. **Hours:** Mon-Sat 9:30-17:00, Sun 12:00-16:45. See page 77.

EDINBURGH

ley (who wears his kilt as if pants don't exist, £150/half-day, £300/ day, extra charge if he uses his car—seats up to six, +44 131 666 1944, mobile +44 771 034 2044, www.small-world-tours.co.uk, kennethhanley@me.com); **Liz Everett** (walking tours only—no car; £190/half-day, £300/day, +44 782 168 3837, liz.everett@live. co.uk); and **Maggie McLeod** (another top-notch guide, £195/ half-day walking tour, £660 day trips with car to farther-flung destinations, +44 775 151 6776, www.scotlandandmore.com, margaret.mcleod@live.co.uk).

Hop-On, Hop-Off Bus Tours

Three one-hour hop-on, hop-off bus tour routes, all run by the same company, circle the town center, stopping at the major sights

(covered by the Royal Edinburgh Ticket described on page 5). **Edinburgh Tour** (green buses) focuses on the city center, with live guides (stay on for the entire 75-minute loop if you like your guide). **City Sightseeing** (red buses, focuses on Old Town) has recorded commentary, as does the **Majestic Tour** (blue-and-yellow buses, goes to the port of Leith and includes a stop at the *Britannia* and Royal Botanic Garden). You can pay for just one tour (£16/24 hours), but most people pay a few pounds more for a ticket covering all buses (£20/24 hours, £24/48 hours). It's a great convenience to be able to hop on any bus that goes by with the same ticket (buses run April-Oct roughly 9:00-19:00, shorter hours off-season; about every 10 minutes, buy tickets on board, +44 131 220 0770, www.edinburghtour.com). On sunny days, the buses go topless. As is generally the case with such tours, there's patter the entire time but almost nothing of real importance other than identifying what you're driving by and a few random factoids (the live guides are little better than the recorded spiels).

The **3 Bridges Tour** combines a hop-on, hop-off bus to South Queensferry with a boat tour on the Firth of Forth (£28, 3 hours total).

Day Trips from Edinburgh

Many companies run a variety of day trips to regional sights, as well as multiday and themed itineraries. (Several of the local guides listed earlier have cars, too.)

The most popular tour is the all-day **Highlands trip,** which gives those with limited time a chance to experience the wonders of Scotland's wild and legend-soaked Highlands in a single long day (about £55-65, roughly 8:00-20:00). Itineraries vary, but you'll generally visit/pass through the Trossachs, Rannoch Moor, Glencoe, Fort William, Fort Augustus on Loch Ness (some tours offer an optional boat ride), and Pitlochry. To save time, look for a tour that gives you a short glimpse of Loch Ness rather than driving its entire length or doing a boat trip. (Once you've seen a little of it, you've seen it all.) Also popular are all-day tours of locations from the *Outlander* novels and TV series (similar price and timing).

Larger outfits, typically using bigger buses, include **Timberbush Tours** (+44 131 226 6066, www.timberbush-tours.co.uk), **Gray Line** (+44 131 555 5558, www.graylinescotland.com), **Highland Experience** (+44 131 226 1414, www.highlandexperience.com), and **Highland Explorer** (+44 131 558 3738, www.highlandexplorertours.com). Other companies pride themselves on keeping group sizes small, with 16-seat minibuses; these include **Rabbie's** (+44 131 226 3133, www.rabbies.com) and **Heart of Scotland Tours: The Wee Red Bus** (RS%—10 percent Rick Steves discount on full-price day tours, mention when booking, does not apply to overnight tours or senior/student rates; may cancel off-season if too few sign up—leave a contact number; +44 131 228 2888, www.heartofscotlandtours.co.uk, run by Nick Roche).

For young backpackers, **Haggis Adventures** runs day tours plus overnight trips of up to 10 days (+44 131 557 9393, www.haggisadventures.com).

At **Discreet Scotland,** Matthew Wight and his partners specialize in tours of greater Edinburgh and Scotland in spacious SUVs—good for families (£485/2 people, 8 hours, +44 798 941 6990, www.discreetscotland.com).

Walks in Edinburgh

I've outlined two walks in Edinburgh: along the Royal Mile, and through the New Town. Many of the sights we'll pass on these walks are described in more detail later, under "Sights in Edinburgh."

THE ROYAL MILE
The Royal Mile is one of Europe's most interesting historic walks (rated ▲▲▲). ∩ Download my free Royal Mile Walk **audio tour** and I'll narrate as you walk.

This 1.5-hour walk covers the Royal Mile's landmarks, but skips the many museums and indoor sights along the way (these are described in walking order under "Sights in Edinburgh" on page 48). Doing this walk as an orientation upon arrival in the early

morning or evening allows you to focus on the past without having to dodge crowds. You can return later to stroll the same walk during the much livelier business hours when shops, museums, and the cathedral are all open.

Another option is to review the sight descriptions beforehand, plan your walk around their open hours, and pop into those that interest you as you pass them. Several of the sights you'll pass on this walk are free to enter, including the Writers' Museum, St. Giles' Cathedral, Old Parliament House, People's Story Museum, Museum of Edinburgh, and Scottish parliament building.

Overview

Start at Edinburgh Castle at the top and amble down to the Palace of Holyroodhouse. The street itself changes names—Castlehill, Lawnmarket, High Street, and Canongate—but it's a straight, downhill shot totaling just over one mile. And

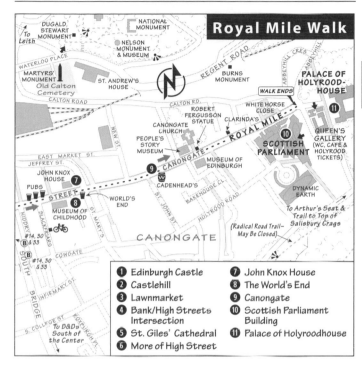

Royal Mile Walk

EDINBURGH

① Edinburgh Castle
② Castlehill
③ Lawnmarket
④ Bank/High Streets Intersection
⑤ St. Giles' Cathedral
⑥ More of High Street
⑦ John Knox House
⑧ The World's End
⑨ Canongate
⑩ Scottish Parliament Building
⑪ Palace of Holyroodhouse

nearly every step is packed with shops, cafés, and lanes leading to tiny squares.

The city of Edinburgh was born on the rock at the top, where the castle stands today. Celtic tribes (and maybe the Romans) once occupied this site. As the town grew, it spilled downhill along the sloping ridge that became the Royal Mile. Because this strip of land is so narrow, there was no place to build but up. So in medieval times, it was densely packed with multistory "tenements"—large edifices under one roof that housed a number of tenants.

As you walk, you'll be tracing the growth of the city—its birth atop Castle Hill, its Old Town heyday in the 1600s, its expansion in the 1700s into the Georgian New Town (leaving the old quarter an overcrowded, disease-ridden Victorian slum), and on to the 21st century at the modern Scottish parliament building (2004).

Most of the Royal Mile feels like one long Scottish shopping mall, selling all manner of kitschy souvenirs (known locally as "tartan tat"), shortbread, and whisky. But the streets are also packed with history, and if you push past the postcard racks into one of the many side alleys, you can still find a few surviving rough edges of the old city. Despite the drizzle, be sure to look up—spires, carvings, and towering Gothic "skyscrapers" give this city its unique urban identity.

As you stroll this mostly traffic-free tourist strip, you'll weave between big military-style barriers designed to frustrate terrorists, and navigate a can-can of low-grade souvenir shops and eateries, tourists with rolling suitcases, and cruise groups following their guides' umbrellas. Along the way, you'll be entertained by buskers, perused by pickpockets, hit up by beggars, and tempted by street merchants. Oh, and as it's quite haunted, you may feel the presence of a few ghosts.

• *We'll start at the castle esplanade, the big parking lot at the entrance to...*

❶ Edinburgh Castle

Edinburgh was born on the bluff—a big rock—where the castle now stands. Since before recorded history, people have lived on this strategic, easily defended perch.

The **castle** is an imposing symbol of Scottish independence (for a self-guided castle tour, see page 37.) Its esplanade—built as a military parade ground (1816)—is now the site of the annual Military Tattoo. This spectacular massing of regimental bands fills the square nightly for most of August. Fans watch from temporary bleacher seats to see kilt-wearing dancers and bagpipers marching against the spectacular backdrop of the castle. (It takes three months to set up the bleachers, so you'll see them, in some form, for most of the summer.) TV crews broadcast the spectacle to all corners of the globe.

When the bleachers aren't up, there are fine views in both directions from the esplanade. Facing north (to the right), you'll see the body of water called the Firth of Forth, and Fife beyond that. (The Firth of Forth is the estuary where the River Forth flows into the North Sea.) Still facing north, find the lacy spire of the Scott Monument and two Neoclassical buildings housing art galleries. Beyond them, the stately buildings of Edinburgh's  New Town rise. Panning to the right, find the Nelson Monument and some faux Greek ruins atop Calton Hill (see page 83).

The city's many bluffs, crags, and ridges were built up by volcanoes, then carved down by glaciers—a city formed in "fire and ice," as the locals say. So, during the Ice Age, as a river of glaciers swept in from the west (behind today's castle), it ran into the super-hard volcanic basalt of Castle Rock and flowed around it, cutting valleys on either side and leaving a tail that became the Royal Mile you're about to walk.

At the bottom of the esplanade, where the square hits the road, look left (with your back to the castle) to find a plaque on the wall above the tiny **witches' well** (now a planter, on the side of the Tartan Weaving Mill). This memorializes 300 women who were accused of witchcraft and burned here. Below was the Nor' Loch, the swampy lake where those accused of witchcraft were bound and dropped into the lake. If they sank and drowned, they were innocent. If they floated, they were guilty, and were burned here in front of the castle, providing the city folk a nice afternoon out. The plaque shows two witches: one good and one bad. Tickle the serpent's snout to sympathize with the witches. (I just made that up.)

• *Start walking down the bustling Royal Mile. The first block is a street called...*

❷ Castlehill

The big, squat, tank-like building immediately on your left was formerly the Old Town's reservoir. While it once held 1.5 million gallons of water, today it's filled with the touristy **Tartan Weaving Mill** (open daily 9:00-17:30), a massive complex of four floors selling every kind of Scottish cliché. At the bottom level (a long way down) is a floor of big looms and weavers sometimes at work.

The black-and-white tower ahead on the left has entertained visitors since the 1850s with its **camera obscura,** a darkened room where a mirror and a series of lenses capture live images of the city surroundings outside. (Giggle at the funny mirrors as you walk fatly by.) Across the street, filling the old Castlehill Primary School, is a gimmicky-if-intoxicating whisky-sampling exhibit called the **Scotch Whisky Experience** (a.k.a. "Malt Disney"). Both are described later, under "Sights in Edinburgh."

• *Just ahead, in front of the church with the tall, lacy spire, is the old market square known as...*

❸ Lawnmarket

During the Royal Mile's heyday, in the 1600s, this intersection was bigger and served as a market for fabric (especially "lawn," a linen-like cloth). The market would fill this space with hustle, bustle, and lots of commerce. The round white hump in the middle of the roundabout is all that remains of the official weighing beam called the Butter Tron—where all goods sold were weighed for honesty and tax purposes.

Towering above Lawnmarket, with the highest spire in the city, is the former Tolbooth Church. This impressive Neo-Gothic structure (1844) is now home to **the Hub,** Edinburgh's festival-ticket and information center. While it's closed much of the year— except for a couple of food trucks out front, during the festivities this is a handy stop for its WC, café, and information. The world-famous Edinburgh Festival fills the month of August with cultural action, while other August festivals feature classical music, tra-ditional and fringe theater (especially com-edy), art, books, and more.

In the 1600s, this—along with the next stretch, called High Street—was the city's main street. At that time, Edinburgh was bursting with breweries, printing presses, and banks. Tens of thou-sands of citizens were squeezed into the narrow confines of the Old Town.

Here on this ridge, they built tenements (multiple-unit resi-dences) similar to the more recent ones you see today. These tene-ments, rising 10 stories and more, were some of the tallest domestic buildings in Europe. The living arrangements shocked class-con-scious English visitors to Edinburgh because the tenements were occupied by rich and poor alike—usually the poor in the cellars and attics, and the rich in the middle floors.

• *Continue a half-block down the Mile.*

Gladstone's Land (at #477b, on the left), a surviving original tenement, was acquired by a wealthy merchant in 1617. Stand in front of the building and look up at this centuries-old skyscraper. This design was standard for its time: a shop or shops on the ground floor, with columns and an arcade, and residences on the floors above. Because window glass was expensive, the lower halves of window openings were made of cheaper wood, which swung out like shutters for ventilation—and were convenient for tossing out garbage. Now a museum, Gladstone's Land is worth visiting for its intimate look at life here 400 years ago (see page 49).

Branching off the spine of the Royal Mile are a number of nar-row alleyways that go by various local names. A "wynd" (rhymes with "kind") is a narrow, winding lane. A "pend" is an arched gate-way. "Gate" is from an Old Norse word for street. And a "close" is a tiny alley between two buildings (originally with a door that "closed" at night). A "close" usually leads to a "court," or courtyard.

To explore one of these alleyways, head into Lady Stair's Close (on the left, 10 steps downhill from Gladstone's Land). This alley pops out in a small courtyard, where you'll find the **Writers' Museum** (described on page 50). It's free and well worth a visit for fans of Scotland's holy trinity of writers (Robert Burns, Sir Walter Scott, and Robert Louis Stevenson), but also for a glimpse of what a typical home might have looked like in the 1600s. Burns actually lived for a while in this neighborhood, in 1786, when he first arrived in Edinburgh. Notice that the courtyard is paved with stones memorializing various Scottish-born writers.

Opposite Gladstone's Land (at #322), another close leads to **Riddle's Court.** Wander through here and imagine Edinburgh in the 17th and 18th centuries, when tourists came here to marvel at its skyscrapers. Some 40,000 people were jammed into the few blocks between here and the World's End pub (which we'll reach soon). Visualize the labyrinthine maze of the old city, with people scurrying through these back alleyways, buying and selling, and popping into taverns.

No city in Europe was as densely populated—or perhaps as filthy. Without modern hygiene, it was a living hell of smoke, stench, and noise, with the constant threat of fire, collapse, and disease. The dirt streets were soiled with sewage from bedpans emptied out windows. By the 1700s, the Old Town was rife with poverty and disease. The smoky home fires rising from tenements and the infamous smell (or "reek" in Scottish) that wafted across the city gave it a nickname that sticks today: "Auld Reekie."

• *Return to the Royal Mile and continue down it a few steps to take in some sights at the...*

❹ Bank/High Streets Intersection

Several sights cluster here, where Lawnmarket changes its name to High Street and intersects with Bank Street and George IV Bridge.

Begin with **Deacon Brodie's Tavern,** on the left corner. Read the "Doctor Jekyll and Mr. Hyde" story of this pub's notorious namesake on the wall facing Bank Street. Then, to see his spooky split personality, check out both sides of the hanging signpost. Brodie—a pillar of the community by day but a burglar by night—epitomizes the divided personality of 1700s Edinburgh. It was a rich, productive city—home to great philosophers and scientists, who actively contributed to the Enlightenment. Meanwhile, the Old Town was riddled with crime and squalor. The city was scandalized when

this respected surgeon—driven by a passion for medical research and needing corpses—was accused of colluding with two low-lifes, named Burke and Hare, to acquire freshly murdered corpses for dissection. (A century later, novelist Robert Louis Stevenson would capture the dichotomy of Edinburgh's rich-poor society—and, perhaps, borrow some specifics from the tale of Brodie himself—in his *Strange Case of Dr. Jekyll and Mr. Hyde*.)

In the late 1700s, Edinburgh's upper class moved out of the Old Town into a planned community called the New Town (a quarter-mile north of here). Eventually, most tenements were torn down and replaced with newer Victorian buildings. You'll see some at this intersection.

Look left down Bank Street to the green-domed **Bank of Scotland.** This was the headquarters of the bank, which had practiced modern capitalist financing since 1695. The building now houses the Museum on the Mound, a free exhibit on banking history (see page 51), and is also the Scottish headquarters for Lloyds Banking Group—which swallowed up the Bank of Scotland after the financial crisis of 2008.

If you detour left down Bank Street toward the bank, you'll find the recommended **Whiski Rooms Shop.** If you head in the opposite direction, down George IV Bridge, you'll reach the **National Library of Scotland** (with its fine and free "Treasures" exhibit), the excellent **National Museum of Scotland,** the famous Greyfriars Bobby statue, photogenic Victoria Street, which leads to the pub-lined Grassmarket square (all described later in this chapter), and several recommended eateries. Victoria Street is so dreamy, many Harry Potter fans figure it must be the inspiration for J. K. Rowling's Diagon Alley.

Across the street from Deacon Brodie's Tavern is a seated green statue of hometown boy **David Hume** (1711-1776)—one of the most influential thinkers not only of Scotland, but in all of Western philosophy. The atheistic Hume was one of the towering figures of the Scottish Enlightenment of the mid-1700s. Thinkers and scientists were using the scientific method to challenge and investigate everything, including religion. Hume questioned cause and effect in thought puzzles such as this: We can see that when one billiard ball strikes another, the second one moves, but how do we know the collision "caused" the movement? Notice his shiny toe: People on their way to trial (in the high court just behind the statue) or stu-

dents on their way to exams (in the nearby university) rub it for good luck.

Follow David Hume's gaze to the opposite corner, where a **brass H** in the pavement marks the site of the last public execution in Edinburgh in 1864. Deacon Brodie himself would have been hung about here (in 1788, on gallows whose design he had helped to improve—smart guy).

• *From the brass H, continue down the Royal Mile, pausing just before the church square at a stone wellhead with the pyramid cap.*

All along the Royal Mile, **wellheads** like this (from 1835) provided townsfolk with water in the days before buildings had plumbing. These neighborhood wells were served by the reservoir up at the castle. Imagine long lines of people in need of water standing here, gossiping and sharing the news. Eventually buildings were retrofitted with water pipes—the ones you see running along building exteriors.

• *Ahead of you (past the Victorian statue of some duke), embedded in the cobblestones near the street, is a big heart.*

The **Heart of Midlothian** marks the spot of the city's 15th-century municipal building and jail. In times past, in a nearby open space, criminals were hanged, traitors were decapitated, and witches were burned. Citizens hated the rough justice doled out here. Locals still spit on the heart in the pavement. Go ahead...do as the locals do—land one right in the heart of the heart. By the way, Edinburgh has two soccer teams—Heart of Midlothian (known as "Hearts") and Hibernian ("Hibs"). If you're a Hibs fan, spit again.

• *Make your way to the entrance of the church.*

❺ St. Giles' Cathedral

This is the flagship of the Church of Scotland (Scotland's largest denomination) called the "Mother Church of Presbyterianism."

The interior serves as a kind of Scottish Westminster Abbey, filled with monuments, statues, plaques, and stained-glass windows dedicated to great Scots and moments in history.

A church has stood on this spot since 854, though this structure is an architectural hodgepodge, dating mostly from the 15th through 19th century. In the 16th century, St. Giles was a kind of national stage on which the drama of the Reformation was played out. The reformer John Knox (1514-1572) was the preacher here. His fiery sermons helped turn once-Catholic Edinburgh into a bastion of Protestantism. During the Scottish Reformation, St. Giles was transformed from a Catholic cathedral to a Presbyterian church. The spacious interior is well worth a visit (for a self-guided tour, see page 51).

• *Facing the church entrance, curl around its right side, into a parking lot.*

Sights Around St. Giles

The grand building across the parking lot from St. Giles is the **Old Parliament House.** Since the 13th century, the king had ruled a rubber-stamp parliament of nobles and bishops. But the Protestant Reformation promoted democracy, and the parliament gained real power. From the early 1600s until 1707, this building evolved to become the seat of a true parliament of elected officials. That came to an end in 1707, when Scotland signed an Act of Union, joining what's known today as the United Kingdom and giving up their right to self-rule. (More on that later in the walk.) If you're curious to peek inside, head through the door at #11 (described on page 55).

The great reformer **John Knox** is buried—with appropriate austerity—under parking lot spot #23. The statue among the cars shows King Charles II riding to a toga party back in 1685.

• *Continue through the parking lot, around the back end of the church.*

Every Scottish burgh (town licensed by the king to trade) had three standard features: a "tolbooth" (basically a Town Hall, with a courthouse, meeting room, and jail); a "tron" (official weighing scale); and a "mercat" (or market) cross. The **mercat cross** standing just behind St. Giles' Cathedral has a slender column decorated with a unicorn holding a flag with the cross of St. Andrew. Royal proclamations have been read at this mercat cross since the 14th century. In 2022, a town crier heralded the news that Britain had a new king—three days after the actual event (traditionally the time it took for a horse to speed here from London). Today, Mercat Cross is the meeting point for many of Edinburgh's walking tours—both historic and ghostly.

• *Circle around to the street side of the church, to the statue at the nearest corner.*

This memorial to **Adam Smith** honors the Edinburgh author of the pioneering *Wealth of Nations* (1776), in which he laid out the economics of free-market capitalism. Smith theorized that an "invisible hand" wisely guides the unregulated free market. Stand in front of Smith and imagine the intellectual energy of Edinburgh in the mid-1700s, when it was Europe's most enlightened city. Adam Smith was right in the center of it. He and David Hume were good friends. James Boswell, the famed biographer of Samuel Johnson, took classes from Smith. James Watt, inventor of the steam engine, was another proud Scotsman of the age. With great intellectuals like these, Edinburgh helped create the modern world. The poet Robert Burns, geologist James Hutton (who's considered the father of modern geology), and the publishers of the first *Encyclopedia Britannica* all lived in Edinburgh. Steeped in the inquisitive mindset of the Enlightenment, they applied cool rationality and a secular approach to their respective fields.

Across the street from Smith, you'll see the entrance to a fun attraction called the Real Mary King's Close (see page 55).
• *Head on down the Royal Mile.*

❻ More of High Street

Continuing down this stretch of the Royal Mile, which is traffic-free most of the day (notice the bollards that raise and lower for permitted traffic), you'll see the Fringe Festival office (on the right, at #180), street musicians, and another wellhead (with horse "sippies," dating from 1675).

Notice those **three red boxes.** In the 20th century, people used these to make telephonic calls to each other. (Imagine that!) These cast-iron booths were produced in Scotland for all of Britain. As phone booths are decommissioned, some are finding new use as tiny shops and ATMs, and even showing up in residential neighborhoods as nostalgic garden decorations.

At the next intersection, on the left, is **Cockburn Street** (pronounced "COE-burn"), with a reputation for its eclectic independent shops and string of trendy bars and eateries. In the Middle Ages, only tiny lanes (like Fleshmarket Close just uphill) interrupted the long line of Royal Mile buildings. Cockburn Street was cut through High Street's dense wall of medieval skyscrapers in the 1860s to give easy access to the Georgian New Town and the train station. Notice how the sliced buildings were thoughtfully capped with facades that fit the aesthetic look of the Royal Mile.
• *When you reach the Tron Church (with a fine 17th-century interior, currently housing history exhibits and shops), you're at the intersection of* **North and South Bridge** *streets. These major streets lead left to Waverley Station and right to the B&B neighborhood south of the center. Several handy bus lines run along here.*

This is the halfway point of this walk. Stand on the corner diagonally across from the church. Look up to the top of the Royal Mile at the Hub and its 240-foot spire. In front of that, take in the spire of St. Giles' Cathedral—inspired by the Scottish crown and the thistle, Scotland's national flower.

With its faux turret and made-up 16th-century charm, the **Radisson Blu Hotel** (on the left) is entirely new construction, dating only from 1990, but built to fit in. The city is protecting its historic look. The **Inn on the Mile,** directly across the street, was once a fancy bank with a lavish interior. As modern banks are moving away from city centers, their sumptuous buildings are being converted into ornate pubs and restaurants.

Continue downhill. In the next block are three **characteristic pubs** (The Mitre, Royal Mile, and Whiski), side by side, that offer free folk music many evenings. On the facing buildings, notice the chimneys. Tenement buildings shared stairways and entries, but held individual apartments, each with its own chimney.

• *Go down High Street another block, passing near the **Museum of Childhood** (on the right, at #42, and worth a stop; see page 55).*

Directly across the street, just below another wellhead, is the...

❼ John Knox House

Remember that Knox was a towering figure in Edinburgh's history, converting Scotland to a Calvinist style of Protestantism. His religious bent was "Presbyterianism," in which parishes are governed by elected officials rather than appointed bishops. This more democratic brand of Christianity also spurred Scotland toward political democracy. If you're interested in Knox or the Reformation, this sight is worth a visit (see page 55). Full disclosure: It's not certain that Knox ever actually lived here. Attached to the Knox House is the Scottish Storytelling Centre, where locals with the gift of gab perform regularly; check the posted schedule.

• *A few steps farther down High Street, at the intersection with St. Mary's and Jeffrey streets, you'll reach...*

❽ The World's End

For centuries, a wall stood here, marking the end of the burgh of Edinburgh. For residents within the protective walls of the city, this must have felt like the "world's end," indeed. You can even pop in for a pint at the recommended The World's End pub, to your right. The area beyond was called Canongate, a monastic community associated with Holyrood Abbey. At the intersection, find the brass bricks in the street that trace the gate (demolished in 1764).

Look to the right down St. Mary's Street about 200 yards to see a surviving bit of that old wall, known as the **Flodden Wall.** In the 1513 Battle of Flodden, the Scottish king James IV made the disastrous decision to invade northern England. James and 10,000 of his Scotsmen were killed. Fearing a brutal English counterattack, Edinburgh scrambled to reinforce its broken-down city wall.

Look left down Jeffrey Street past the train tracks for a good view of **Old Calton Cemetery** up on Calton Hill. The obelisk,

called Martyrs' Monument, remembers a group of 18th-century patriots exiled by London to Australia for their reform politics. The round building to the left is the grave of philosopher David Hume. Today, the main reason to go up Calton Hill is for the fine views (see page 83).

• *Continue down the Royal Mile—leaving old Edinburgh—as High Street changes names to...*

❾ Canongate

A couple blocks farther along (on the right at #172) you reach **Cadenhead's,** a serious whisky shop (see page 89). Beyond that, you'll pass two worthwhile and free museums, the **People's Story Museum** (on the left, in the old tollhouse at #163) and the **Museum of Edinburgh** (on the right, at #142), with the entry to the characteristic Bakehouse Close next door (for more on all three, see pages 57 and 58). But our next stop is the church just across from the Museum of Edinburgh.

The 1688 **Canongate Kirk** (Church)—located not far from the royal residence of Holyroodhouse—is where the royal family worship whenever they're in town. (So don't sit in the front pew, marked with a crown.) The gilded emblem at the top of the roof, high above the door, has the antlers of a stag from the royal estate of Balmoral.

The church is open only when volunteers have signed up to welcome visitors. Chat them up and borrow the description of the place. Then step inside the lofty blue and red interior, renovated with royal money; the church is filled with light and the flags of various Scottish regiments. In the narthex, peruse the photos of royal family events here, and find the list of priests and ministers of this parish—it goes back to 1143 (with a clear break with the Reformation in 1561).

Outside, turn right as you leave the church and walk up into the graveyard. The large, gated grave (abutting the back of the People's Story Museum) is the affectionately tended tomb of **Adam Smith,** the father of capitalism. (Throw him a penny or two.)

The statue on the sidewalk in front of the church is of the poet **Robert Fergusson.** One of the first to write verse in the Scots language, he so inspired Robert Burns that Burns paid for Fergusson's tombstone in the Canongate churchyard and composed his epitaph.

Now look across the street at the **gabled house** next to the Museum of Edinburgh. Scan the facade to see shells placed there in the 17th century to defend against the evil power of witches yet to be drowned.

• *Walk about 300 yards farther along (past the recommended* **Clarinda's Tea Room***). In the distance you can see the Palace of Holyroodhouse (the end of this walk) and soon, on the right, you'll come to the modern Scottish parliament building.*

Just opposite the parliament building is **White Horse Close** (on the left; passage marked *27* in the white arcade that juts out over the sidewalk). Step into this 17th-century courtyard. It was from here that the Edinburgh stagecoach left for London. Eight days later, the horse-drawn carriage would pull into its destination: Scotland Yard. Note that bus #35 leaves in two directions from here—downhill for the Royal Yacht *Britannia,*

and uphill along the Royal Mile (as far as South Bridge) and on to the National Museum of Scotland.

• *Now walk up around the corner to the flagpoles (flying the flags of Europe, Britain, and Scotland) in front of the...*

⑩ Scottish Parliament Building

Finally, after centuries of history, we reach the 21st century. And finally, after three centuries of London rule, Scotland has a parliament building...in Scotland. When Scotland united with England in 1707, its parliament was dissolved. But in 1999, the Scottish parliament was reestablished, and in 2004, it moved into this striking home. Notice how the eco-friendly building, by the Catalan architect Enric Miralles, mixes wild angles,

lots of light, bold windows, oak, and native stone into a startling complex. (People from Catalunya—another would-be breakaway nation—have an affinity for Scotland.) From the front of the parliament building, look in the distance at the rocky Salisbury Crags, where people hike the traverse up to the dramatic next summit called Arthur's Seat. Now look at the building in relation to the craggy cliffs. The architect envisioned the building as if it were rising right from the base of Arthur's Seat, almost bursting from the rock.

Since it celebrates Scottish democracy, the architecture is not a statement of authority. There are no statues of old heroes. There's not even a grand entry. You feel like you're entering an office park. Given its neighborhood, the media often calls the Scottish Parliament "Holyrood" for short (similar to calling the US Congress "Capitol Hill"). For details on touring the building and seeing parliament in action, see page 58.

• *Across the street is the **Queen's Gallery**, with a sampling of the late Queen Elizabeth II's personal art collection (see page 61). Finally, walk to the end of the road (Abbey Strand), and step up to the impressive wrought-iron gate of the palace. Look up at the stag with its holy cross, or "holy rood," on its forehead, and peer into the palace grounds. (The ticket office and palace entryway, a fine café, and a handy WC are just through the arch on the right.)*

⓫ Palace of Holyroodhouse

Since the 16th century, this palace has marked the end of the Royal Mile. An abbey—part of a 12th-century Augustinian monastery—originally stood in its place. While most of that old building is gone, you can see the surviving nave behind the palace on the left. According to one legend, it was named "holy rood" for a piece of the cross, brought here as a relic by Queen (and later

Saint) Margaret. (Another version of the story is that King David I, Margaret's son, saw the image of a cross upon a stag's head while hunting here and took it as a sign that he should build an abbey on the site.) Because Scotland's royalty preferred living at Holyroodhouse to the blustery castle on the rock, the palace grew over time. If the royal family's not visiting, the palace welcomes visitors (get tickets in the Queen's Gallery; see page 61 for details).

• *Your walk—from the castle to the palace, with so much Scottish history*

New Town Walk: Georgian Edinburgh

200 Meters
200 Yards

To Leith

RIVERSIDE PATH

Water of Leith

Moray Place

Queen

QUEEN

NEW

Ainslie Place

ST. COLME ST.

GEORGIAN HOUSE

WALK ENDS

Charlotte Square

HOPE ST.

HOPE ST. LANE

QUEENSFERRY ST.

RIATTA ST.

SHANDWICK PL.

To Haymarket Station

EDINBURGH GIN DISTILLERY

WALDORF ASTORIA

WEST END

GLOUCESTER LN.

INDIA ST.

JAMAICA

HOWE ST.

GARDENS W.

QUEEN ST.

GARDENS E.

HERIOT ROW

HILL ST.

HILL ST. N. LANE

HILL ST. S. LANE

YOUNG ST. N. LANE

YOUNG ST.

YOUNG ST. S. LANE

S CHARLOTTE ST.

CASTLE ST.

GEORGE STREET

ROSE ST. N. LANE

ROSE ST.

ROSE ST. S. LANE

ROSE

PRINCES

ST. CUTHBERT'S

EDINBURGH CASTLE

1. View from Waverly Bridge
2. Princes Street Gardens
3. Scott Monument
4. Former Jenners Dep't Store
5. St. Andrew Square
6. George Street
7. St. Andrew's & St. George's Church
8. The Dome Restaurant
9. King George IV Statue
10. Thistle Street
11. William Pitt Statue
12. Rose Street
13. Charlotte Square
14. Georgian House

packed in between—is complete. But if your appetite is whetted, don't worry, there's much more to see. Enjoy the rest of Edinburgh.

NEW TOWN WALK: GEORGIAN EDINBURGH

Many visitors, mesmerized by the Royal Mile, never venture to the New Town. And that's a shame. With the city's finest Georgian architecture (from its 18th-century boom period), the New Town has a completely different character than the Old Town. This self-guided walk—worth ▲▲—gives you a quick orientation in about one hour.

• *Begin on Waverley Bridge, spanning the gully between the Old and New towns; to get there from the Royal Mile, just head down the curved Cockburn Street near the Tron Church (or cut down any of the "close" lanes opposite St. Giles Cathedral). Stand on the bridge overlooking the train tracks, facing the castle.*

1 View from Waverley Bridge: From this vantage point, you can enjoy fine views of medieval Edinburgh, with its 10-story-plus "skyscrapers." It's easy to imagine how miserably crowded this area was, prompting the expansion of the city during the Georgian period.

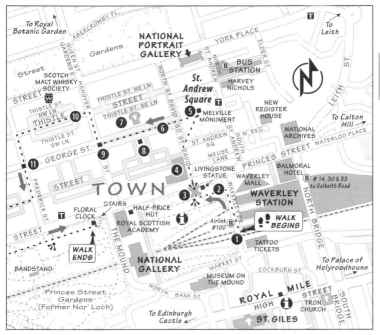

Pick out landmarks along the Royal Mile, most notably the open-work "thistle steeple" of St. Giles.

A big lake called the **Nor' Loch** once was to the north (nor') of the Old Town; now it's a valley between Edinburgh's two towns. The lake was drained around 1800 as part of the expansion. Before that, the lake was the town's water reservoir...and its sewer. Much has been written about the town's infamous stink. The town's nickname, "Auld Reekie," referred to both the smoke of its industry and the stench of its squalor.

The long-gone loch was also a handy place for drowning witches. With their thumbs tied to their ankles, they'd be lashed to dunking stools. Those who survived the ordeal were considered "aided by the devil" and burned as witches. If they died, they were innocent and given a good Christian burial. Edinburgh was Europe's witch-burning mecca—any perceived "sign," including a small birthmark, could condemn you. Scotland burned more witches per capita than any other country—17,000 souls between 1479 and 1722.

Facing the Old Town, look right and visually trace the train tracks as they disappear into a tunnel below the **Scottish National Gallery** (with the best collection anywhere of Scottish paintings; you can visit it during this walk—see page 67). The two fine Neo-classical buildings of the National Gallery date from the 1840s and sit upon a mound that's called...**The Mound.** When the New

Town was built, tons of rubble from the excavations were piled here (1781-1830), forming a dirt bridge that connected the new development with the Old Town to allay merchant concerns about being cut off from the future heart of the city.

Turning 180 degrees (and facing the ramps down into the train station), notice the huge, turreted building with the clock tower. (The clock is famously four minutes fast to help locals not miss their trains.) **The Balmoral** was one of the city's two grand hotels during its glory days (its opposite bookend, the **Waldorf Astoria Edinburgh,** sits at the far end of the former lakebed—near the end of this walk). Aristocrats arriving by train could use a hidden entrance to go from the platform directly up to their plush digs. (Today The Balmoral is known mostly as the place where J. K. Rowling completed the final Harry Potter book. She has a suite there that she uses when struggling with writer's block.)

• *Now walk across the bridge toward the New Town. Before the corner, enter the gated gardens on the left, and head toward the big, pointy monument. You're at the edge of...*

❷ **Princes Street Gardens:** This grassy park, filling the former lakebed, offers a wonderful escape from the bustle of the city. Once the private domain of the wealthy, it was opened to the public around 1870—not as a democratic gesture, but in hopes of increasing sales at the Princes Street department stores (including the now-closed Jenners). Join the office workers for a picnic lunch break.

• *Take a seat on the bench as encouraged by the statue of Livingstone (Dr. Livingstone, I presume?). The Victorian explorer is well equipped with a guidebook but is hardly packing light—his lion skin doesn't even fit in his rucksack carry-on.*

Look up at the towering...

❸ **Scott Monument:** Built in the early 1840s, this elaborate Neo-Gothic monument honors the great author Sir Walter Scott, one of Edinburgh's many illustrious sons. When Scott died in 1832, it was said that "Scotland never owed so much to one man." Scott almost singlehandedly created the image of the Scotland we know. Just as the country was in danger of being assimilated into England, Scott celebrated traditional songs, legends, myths, architecture, and kilts, thereby reviving the Highland culture and cementing a national identity. And, as the father of the Romantic historical novel, he contributed to Western literature in general. Nicknamed "the Gothic Rocket," this 200-foot-tall monument shelters a marble statue of Scott and his favorite pet, Maida, a deerhound who was one of 30 canines this dog lover owned during his lifetime. Climbing the tight, stony spiral staircase of 220 steps earns you a peek at a tiny museum midway and a fine city view at the top (£8, open daily 10:00-17:00, Oct-March until 16:00; 30-minute tours depart on the half hour, last tour 30 minutes before closing; +44 131 529 4068).

• *Exit the park and head across busy Princes Street to the...*

❹ **Former Jenners Department Store:** As you wait for the light to change, notice how statues of women support the build-

ing—just as real women once supported the business. The arrival of new fashions here was such a big deal in the old days that they'd announce it by flying flags on the Nelson Monument atop Calton Hill (which you can see in the distance on the right).

But Jenners began to struggle in the age of online shopping. After 183 years of continuous operation, it closed its doors during the Covid-19 lockdown...and never reopened. Plans call for refurbishment of this historic building, likely with a new tenant.

• *Walk straight up South St. David Street. At the top of the block, kitty-corner on your right, you'll see...*

❺ **St. Andrew Square:** This green space is dedicated to the patron saint of Scotland. In the early 19th century, there were no

shops around here—just fine residences; this was a private garden for the fancy people living here. Now open to the public, the square is a popular lunch hangout for workers. The Melville Monument honors a powermonger member of parliament who, for four decades (around 1800), was nicknamed the "uncrowned king of Scotland."

One block beyond the top of the park on Queen Street is the excellent **Scottish National Portrait Gallery,** which introduces you to the biggest names in Scottish history (see page 72).

• *Follow the Melville Monument's gaze straight ahead out of the park. Cross the street and stand at the top of...*

❻ George Street: This is the main drag of Edinburgh's grid-planned New Town. Laid out in 1776, when King George III was busy putting down a revolution in a troublesome overseas colony, the New Town was a model of urban planning in its day. The architectural style is "Georgian"—British for "Neoclassical." And the street plan came with an unambiguous message: to celebrate the union of Scotland with England into the United Kingdom. (This was particularly important, since Scotland was just two decades removed from the failed Jacobite uprising of Bonnie Prince Charlie.)

If you look at a map, you'll see the politics in the street plan: St. Andrew Square (patron saint of Scotland) and Charlotte Square (George III's queen) bookend the New Town, with its three main streets named for the royal family of the time (George, Queen, and Princes). Thistle and Rose streets—which we'll see near the end of this walk—are named for the national flowers of Scotland and England.

The plan for the New Town was the masterstroke of the 23-year-old urban designer James Craig. George Street—20 feet wider than the others (so a four-horse carriage could make a U-turn)—was the main drag. Running down the high spine of the area, it afforded grand, unobstructed views. As you stroll down George Street, you'll notice that, with Craig's grid, grand cross streets come with fine Old Town and river views to the left and right, and monuments seem placed to accentuate the perspectives.

• *Halfway down the first block of George Street, on the right, is...*

❼ St. Andrew's and St. George's Church: Designed as part of the New Town plan in the 1780s, the church is a product of the Scottish Enlightenment. It has an elliptical plan (the first in Britain) so that all can focus on the pulpit. If it's open, step inside. The church conveys the idea that God is space, light, reason, and ordered beauty. A fine leaflet tells the story of the church, and a handy cafeteria downstairs serves cheap and cheery lunches.

• *Directly across the street from the church is another temple, this one devoted to money.*

❽ The Dome: This former bank building now houses a recommended restaurant; consider ducking inside to view the stunning domed atrium. Its pediment is filled with figures demonstrating various ways to make money, which they do with all the nobility of classical gods.

• *Continue down George Street to the intersection with a statue.*

❾ Statue of King George IV: This statue commemorates George IV's visit to Edinburgh in 1822. Notice the particularly fine axis formed by this cross-street: The National Gallery lines up perfectly with the Royal Mile's skyscrapers and the former Tol-

booth Church, creating a Gotham City collage. If you look in the opposite direction, you'll see the Firth of Forth glimmering in the distance—a reminder of how close Edinburgh is to the sea.

• *By now you've gotten your New Town bearings. Feel free to stop this walk here: If you were to turn left and head down Hanover Street, in a block you'd run into the* **Scottish National Gallery;** *the street behind it curves back up to the Royal Mile.*

But to see more of the New Town—including the Georgian House, offering an insightful look inside one of these fine 18th-century homes— stick with me for a few more long blocks, zigzagging through side streets to see the various personalities that inhabit this rigid grid.

Cross over Hanover Street, turn right, and walk along Hanover just one (short) block. Turn left down...

❿ Thistle Street: Of the many streets in the New Town, this has perhaps the most vivid Scottish character. And that's fitting, as it's named after Scotland's national flower. At the beginning and end of the street, also notice that Craig's street plan included tranquil cul-de-sacs within the larger blocks. Thistle Street seems sleepy, but holds characteristic boutiques and good restaurants (see "Eating in Edinburgh," later).

• *You'll soon reach Frederick Street. Turn left and head toward the...*

⓫ Statue of William Pitt the Younger: Pitt was a prime minister under King George III during the French Revolution and the Napoleonic Wars. His father gave his name to the American city of Pittsburgh (which Scots pronounce as "Pitts-burrah"...I assume).

• *For an interesting contrast, we'll continue down another side street. Carrying on past the statue of Pitt (heading toward Edinburgh Castle), turn right onto...*

⓬ Rose Street: As a rose is to a thistle, and as England is to Scotland, so is brash, boisterous Rose Street to sedate, thoughtful Thistle Street. This stretch of Rose Street feels more commercialized, jammed with chain stores. The far end is packed with pubs and restaurants. As you walk, keep an eye out for the cobbled Tudor rose embedded in the brick sidewalk. When you cross the

aptly named Castle Street, linger over the grand views to Edinburgh Castle. It's almost as if they planned it this way...just for the views.

• *Popping out at the far end of Rose Street, across the street and to your right is...*

➍ **Charlotte Square:** The building of the New Town started cheap with St. Andrew Square, but finished well with this stately space. In 1791, the Edinburgh town coun-cil asked the prestigious Scottish architect Robert Adam to pump up the design for Charlotte Square. The council hoped that Adam's plan would answer criticism that the New Town buildings lacked innovation or ambition—and they got what they wanted. Adam's design, which raised the standard of New Town architecture to "international class," created Edinburgh's finest Georgian square. To this day, the fine garden filling the square is private, reserved for residents only.

• *Along the right side of Charlotte Square, at #7, you can visit the* ➎ *Georgian House, which gives you a great peek be-hind these harmonious Neoclassical facades (see page 75).*

When you're done touring the house, you can head back through the New Town grid, perhaps taking some different streets than the way you came. If you're staying in the West End, you're just a few blocks away from your hotel. Or, for a restful return to our starting point, consider this...

Return Through Princes Street Gardens: From Charlotte Square, drop down to busy Princes Street (noticing the red build-ing to the right—the grand Waldorf Astoria Hotel and twin sister of The Balmoral at the start of our walk). But rather than walk-ing along the busy bus-and-tram-lined shopping drag, head into **Princes Street Gardens** (cross Princes Street and enter the gate on the left). With the castle looming overhead on your right, walk back toward The Mound. You'll pass a playground, a fanciful Vic-torian fountain, more monuments to great Scots, war memorials, and a bandstand (which hosts Scottish country dancing—see page 93). Finally, you'll reach a staircase up to the Scottish National Gallery (though access from this entrance may be limited); and the oldest **floral clock** in the world—perhaps telling you it's time for a spot of tea.

• *Our walk is over. From here, you can tour the gallery; head up Bank Street just behind it to reach the Royal Mile; hop on a bus along Princes Street to your next stop (or B&B); or continue through another stretch of the Princes Street Gardens to the Scott Monument and our starting point.*

Sights in Edinburgh

▲▲▲EDINBURGH CASTLE

The fortified birthplace of the city 1,300 years ago, this imposing symbol of Edinburgh sits proudly on a rock high above the town.

The home of Scotland's kings and queens for centuries, the castle has witnessed royal births, medieval pageantry, and bloody sieges. Today it's a complex of various buildings, the oldest dating from the 12th century, linked by cobbled roads that survive from its more recent use as a military garrison. The castle—with expansive views, plenty of history, and the stunning crown jewels of Scotland—is a fascinating and multifaceted sight.

Cost and Hours: £18 for timed-entry ticket—book online in advance to ensure entry; daily 9:30-18:00, Oct-March until 17:00, last entry one hour before closing; +44 131 225 9846, www.edinburghcastle.scot.

Advance Tickets Recommended: It's smart to book a time slot for your castle visit in advance—it's cheaper and you'll be sure to get in. You must show a printed ticket to enter: Either print it at home or your hotel, or pick it up at the black kiosk just below the esplanade (facing the Tartan Weaving Mill) before joining the castle crowds.

Advance Booking for Sightseeing Passes: Even with a Historic Scotland Explorer Pass or Royal Edinburgh Ticket (described on page 5), which both cover castle entry, you'll need to book an entry time in advance.

When to Go: The castle is usually less crowded after 15:00.

Getting There: Simply walk up the Royal Mile (if arriving by bus from the B&B area south of the city, get off at South Bridge and huff up the Mile for about 15 minutes). Taxis get you closer, dropping you a block below the esplanade at the Hub/Tolbooth Church.

Tours: The castle may offer free, 30-minute introductory **tours** (if running, these depart from Argyle Battery; see clock for next departure). If the tours aren't running, staff stationed around the castle can answer questions. You can also rent an informative

EDINBURGH

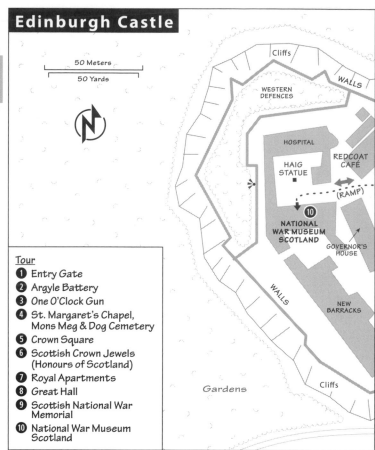

Edinburgh Castle

50 Meters
50 Yards

Cliffs

WALLS

WESTERN
DEFENCES

HOSPITAL

REDCOAT
CAFÉ

HAIG
STATUE

(RAMP)

10
NATIONAL
WAR MUSEUM
SCOTLAND

GOVERNOR'S
HOUSE

WALLS

NEW
BARRACKS

Gardens

Cliffs

Tour
1 Entry Gate
2 Argyle Battery
3 One O'Clock Gun
4 St. Margaret's Chapel,
   Mons Meg & Dog Cemetery
5 Crown Square
6 Scottish Crown Jewels
   (Honours of Scotland)
7 Royal Apartments
8 Great Hall
9 Scottish National War
   Memorial
10 National War Museum
   Scotland

audioguide with four hours of descriptions, including the National War Museum Scotland (£3.50, pick up inside Portcullis Gate).

Eating: The **$ Redcoat Café**—just past the Argyle Battery— is a big, bright, efficient cafeteria with great views. On Crown Square, you'll find **$$ tea rooms** with table service, lunches, and afternoon tea.

⊙ Self-Guided Tour

While important and fun to tour, seeing the castle's highlights— described on this tour—takes only about 1.5 hours.

1 Entry Gate: Approaching from the esplanade, you're greet- ed by the two greatest Scottish heroes. Flanking the entryway are statues of the fierce warriors who battled English invaders, Wil- liam Wallace (on the right) and Robert the Bruce (left). Between them is the Scottish motto, *Nemo me impune lacessit*—roughly, "No one messes with me and gets away with it."

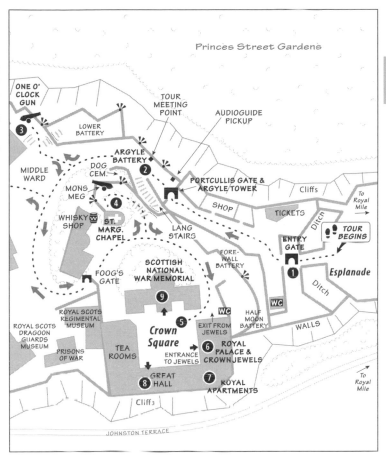

Once inside, start winding your way uphill toward the main sights—the crown jewels and the Royal Palace—located near the summit. Since the castle was protected on three sides by sheer cliffs, the main defense had to be here at the entrance. During the castle's heyday in the 1500s, a 100-foot tower loomed overhead, facing the city.

• *Passing through the **portcullis gate**, you reach the...*

❷ **Argyle (Six-Gun) Battery, with View:** These front-loading, cast-iron cannons are from the Napoleonic era, around 1800, when the castle was still a force to be reckoned with.

From here, look north across the valley to the grid

of the New Town. The valley (directly below) sits where the Nor' Loch once was; this lake was drained and filled in when the New Town was built in the late 1700s, its swamps replaced with gardens. Later the land provided sites for the Greek-temple-esque Scottish National Gallery (above the train line tunnels), Waverley Station (with its glass roof), and the tall, lacy Sir Walter Scott Memorial. Looking farther north, you can make out the port town of Leith (facing the island of Inchkeith), the Firth of Forth, and—in the far, far distance (to the extreme right)—the cone-like mountain of North Berwick Law, a former volcano.

Now look down. The sheer north precipice looks impregnable. But on the night of March 14, 1314, 30 armed men silently scaled this rock face. They were loyal to Robert the Bruce and determined to recapture the castle, which had fallen into English hands. They caught the English by surprise, took the castle, and—three months later—Bruce defeated the English at the Battle of Bannockburn.

Looking back at the gate you just entered, the curved stairway to the right known as Lang Stairs leads steeply up to St. Margaret's Chapel and Crown Square—where we'll end up eventually. But we'll take a more gradual approach.

• *A little farther along, to the right of the Redcoat Café, is the...*

❸ **One O'Clock Gun:** Crowds gather for the 13:00 gun blast (which comes with a little military ceremony), a tradition that gives ships in the bay something to set their navigational devices by. Before the gun, sailors set their clocks with help from the Nelson Monument—that's the tall pillar in the distance on Calton Hill. The monument has a "time ball" affixed to the cross on top, which drops precisely at the top of the hour. But on foggy days, ships couldn't see the ball, so the cannon shot was instituted instead (1861). The tradition stuck, every day at 13:00. (Locals joke that the frugal Scots don't fire it at high noon, as that would cost 11 extra rounds a day.) For more information, there's a small exhibit just down the stairs.

• *Continue uphill, winding to the left and passing through* **Foog's Gate**. *At the very top of the hill, climb up the stairs on your left to reach...*

❹ **St. Margaret's Chapel:** This tiny stone chapel is Edinburgh's oldest building (around 1120) and sits atop its highest point (440 feet). It represents the birth of the city.

In 1057, Malcolm III murdered King Macbeth (of Shakespeare fame) and assumed the Scottish throne. Later, he married Princess Margaret, and the family settled atop this hill. Their marriage united Malcolm's Highland Scots with Margaret's Lowland Anglo-Saxons—the cultural mix that would define Edinburgh.

Step inside the tiny, unadorned church—a testament to Margaret's reputed piety. The elegant-yet-simple stone structure is Romanesque. The nave is wonderfully simple, with classic Norman zigzags decorating the round arch that separates the tiny nave from the sacristy. You'll see a facsimile of St. Margaret's 11th-century gospel book. The small (19th-century Victorian) stained-glass windows feature St. Margaret herself, St. Columba, St. Ninian (who brought Christianity to Scotland in AD 397), St. Andrew (Scotland's patron saint), and William Wallace (the defender of Scotland). These days, the place is popular for weddings. (As it seats only 20, it's particularly popular with parents funding the festivities.)

Margaret died at the castle in 1093, and her son King David I built this chapel in her honor (she was sainted in 1250). David expanded the castle and also founded Holyrood Abbey, across town. These two structures were soon linked by a Royal Mile of buildings, and Edinburgh was born.

Mons Meg, in front of the church, is a huge and once-upon-a-time frightening 15th-century siege cannon that fired 330-pound stones nearly two miles. Look at the huge granite cannon balls and imagine. It was a gift from Philip the Good, duke of

Burgundy, to his great-niece's husband King James II of Scotland.

Nearby, belly up to the banister and look down to find the Dog Cemetery, a tiny patch of grass with a sweet little line of doggie tombstones, marking the graves of soldiers' faithful canine in-arms.

• *Head back down the stairs and carry on straight ahead, along more cannons. Curve right around the big building to enter...*

❺ **Crown Square:** This courtyard is the center of today's Royal Castle complex. Get oriented. You're surrounded by the crown jewels, the Royal Palace (with its Great Hall), and the Scottish National War Memorial.

The castle has evolved over the centuries, and Crown Square is relatively "new." After the time of Malcolm and Margaret,

the castle was greatly expanded by David II (1324-1371), complete with tall towers, a Great Hall, dungeon, cellars, and so on. This served as the grand royal residence for two centuries. Then, in 1571-1573, the Protestant citizens of Edinburgh laid siege to the castle and its Catholic/monarchist holdouts, eventually blasting an earlier castle to smithereens. The palace was rebuilt nearby—around what is today's Crown Square.

• *We'll tour the buildings around Crown Square. First up: the crown jewels, on your left.*

The main entrance, on Crown Square, deposits you straight into the room with the crown jewels but often has a long line. There may be a secondary entrance, around the left side (near the WCs), which takes you—at a shuffle—to the jewels the long way round, through the interesting, Disney-esque "Honours of Scotland" exhibit, which tells the story of the crown jewels and how they survived the harrowing centuries. (If this is not open, just use the main door.)

❻ Scottish Crown Jewels: For centuries, Scotland's monarchs were crowned in elaborate rituals involving three wondrous objects: a jewel-studded crown, scepter, and sword. These objects—along with the ceremonial Stone of Scone (pronounced "skoon")—are known as the "Honours of Scotland." Scotland's crown jewels may not be as impressive as England's, but locals treasure them as a symbol of Scottish nationalism. They're also older than England's; while Oliver Cromwell destroyed England's jewels, the Scots managed to hide theirs.

History of the Jewels: If you're able to see the Honours of Scotland exhibit, you'll learn about the evolution of the jewels, the ceremony, and the often-turbulent journey of this precious regalia. Either way, here's the short version (to read while you're waiting in line):

In 1306, Robert the Bruce was crowned with a "circlet of gold" in a ceremony at Scone—a town 40 miles north of Edinburgh, which Scotland's earliest kings had claimed as their capital. Around 1500, King James IV added two new items to the coronation ceremony—a scepter (a gift from the pope) and a huge sword (a gift from another pope). In 1540, James V had the original crown augmented by an Edinburgh goldsmith, giving it the imperial-crown shape it has today.

These Honours were used to crown every monarch: ninemonth-old Mary, Queen of Scots (she cried); her one-year-old son

William Wallace (c. 1270-1305)

In 1286, Scotland's king died without an heir, plunging the prosperous country into a generation of chaos. As Scottish nobles bickered over naming a successor, the English King Edward I—nicknamed "Longshanks" because of his long legs—invaded and assumed power (1296). He placed a figurehead on the throne, forced Scottish nobles to sign a pledge of allegiance to England (the "Ragman's Roll"), moved the British parliament north to York, and took the highly symbolic Stone of Scone to London, where it would remain for centuries.

WILLIAM WALLACE.

A year later, the Scots rose up against Edward, led by William Wallace. A mix of history and legend portrays Wallace as the son of a poor-but-knightly family that refused to sign the Ragman's Roll. Exceptionally tall and strong, he learned Latin and French from two uncles, who were priests. In his teenage years, his father and older brother were killed by the English. Later, he killed an English sheriff to avenge the death of his wife, Marion. Wallace's rage inspired his fellow Scots to revolt.

In the summer of 1297, Wallace and his guerrillas scored a series of stunning victories over the English. On September 11, a well-equipped English army of 10,000 soldiers and 300 horsemen began crossing Stirling Bridge. Wallace's men attacked, and in the chaos, the bridge collapsed, splitting the English ranks in two. The ragtag Scots drove the confused English into the river. The Battle of Stirling Bridge was a rout, and Wallace was knighted and appointed guardian of Scotland.

All through the winter, King Edward's men chased Wallace, continually frustrated by the Scots' hit-and-run tactics. Finally, at the Battle of Falkirk (1298), they drew Wallace's men out onto the open battlefield. The English with their horses and archers easily destroyed the spear-carrying Scots. Wallace resigned in disgrace and went on the lam, while his successors negotiated truces with the English, finally surrendering unconditionally in 1304. Wallace alone held out.

In 1305, the English tracked him down and took him to London, where he was convicted of treason and mocked with a crown of oak leaves as the "king of outlaws." On August 23, they stripped him naked and dragged him to the execution site. There he was strangled to near death, castrated, and dismembered. His head was stuck on a spike atop London Bridge, while his body parts were sent on tour to spook would-be rebels. But Wallace's martyrdom only served to inspire his countrymen, and Robert the Bruce picked up the torch of independence (see page 47).

James VI (future king of England); and Charles I and II. But the days of divine-right rulers were numbered.

In 1649, the parliament had Charles I (king of both England and Scotland) beheaded. Soon Cromwell's rabid English antiroyalists were marching on Edinburgh. Quick! Hide the jewels! Legend says two women scooped up the crown and sword, hid them in their skirts, and buried them in a church far to the northeast until the coast was clear.

When the monarchy was restored, the regalia were used to crown Scotland's last king, Charles II (1660). Then, in 1707, the Treaty of Union with England ended Scotland's independence. The Honours came out for a ceremony to bless the treaty, and were then locked away in a strongbox in the castle. There they lay for over a century, until Sir Walter Scott—the writer and great champion of Scottish tradition—forced a detailed search of the castle in 1818. The box was found...and there the Honours were, perfectly preserved. Within a few years, they were put on display, as they have been ever since.

The crown's most recent official appearance was in 1999, when it was taken across town to the grand opening of the reinstated parliament, marking a new chapter in the Scottish nation. As it represents the monarchy, the crown is present whenever a new session of parliament opens. (And if Scotland ever secedes, you can be sure that crown will be in the front row.)

The Honours: Finally, you enter the Crown Room to see the regalia itself. The four-foot steel **sword** was made in Italy under orders of Pope Julius II (the man who also commissioned Michelangelo's Sistine Chapel and St. Peter's Basilica). The **scepter** is made of silver, covered with gold, and topped with a rock crystal and a pearl. The gem- and pearl-encrusted **crown** has an imperial arch topped with a cross. Legend says the band of gold in the center is the original crown that once adorned the head of Robert the Bruce.

The **Stone of Scone** (a.k.a. the "Stone of Destiny") sits plain and strong next to the jewels. It's a rough-hewn gray slab of sandstone, about 26 by 17 by 10 inches. As far back as the ninth century, Scotland's kings were crowned atop this stone, when it stood at the medieval capital of Scone. But in 1296, the invading army of Edward I of England carried the stone off to Westminster Abbey. For the next seven centuries, English (and subsequently British) kings and queens were crowned sitting on a coronation chair with the Stone of Scone tucked in a compartment underneath.

In 1950, four Scottish students broke into Westminster Abbey on Christmas Day and smuggled the stone back to Scotland in an act of foolhardy patriotism. But what could they do with it? After three months, they abandoned the stone, draped in Scotland's national flag. It was returned to Westminster Abbey, where (in 1953) Queen Elizabeth II was crowned atop it. In 1996, in recognition of increased Scottish autonomy, Elizabeth agreed to let the stone go home, on one condition: that it be returned to Westminster Abbey for all British coronations.

• *Exit the crown jewel display, heading down the stairs. But just before exiting into the courtyard, turn left through a door that leads into the...*

❼ **Royal Apartments:** Scottish royalty lived in the Royal Palace only when safety or protocol required it (they preferred

the Palace of Holyroodhouse at the bottom of the Royal Mile). Here you can see several rooms that are historic, if not quite thrilling. From the main room where you enter, you can peek into the smaller, wood-paneled room labeled *Birthplace of James VI*—where Mary, Queen of Scots (1542-1587) gave birth to James VI of Scotland, who later became King James I of England. Farther along, **Laich Hall** (Lower Hall) was the dining room of the royal family.

• *Head back outside, turn left across the square, and find the entry on the left to the...*

❽ **Great Hall:** Built by James IV to host the castle's official banquets and meetings, the Great Hall is still used for such purpos-

es today. Most of the interior—its fireplace, carved walls, pikes, and armor—is Victorian. But the well-constructed wood ceiling is original. This hammer-beam roof (constructed like the hull of a ship) is self-supporting. The complex system of braces and arches distributes the weight of the roof outward to the walls, so there's no need for supporting pillars or long cross beams. Before leaving, look for the tiny iron-barred window above the fireplace, on the right. This allowed the king to spy on his subjects while they partied.

• *Back outside, across the Crown Square courtyard is the...*

❾ **Scottish National War Memorial:** This commemorates the

149,000 Scottish soldiers lost in World War I, the 58,000 who died in World War II, and the nearly 800 (and counting) lost in British battles since. Before entering, notice how the Art Deco facade (built in the 1920s with the historic stones of a church that once stood on this spot) fits perfectly with the surrounding buildings.

Inside, the main memorial is directly ahead, but you'll turn right and circulate counterclockwise. Since this structure was built after World War I, the scenes in the windows are from that war. Memorials honor regiments from each of the four branches of the British military with maroon remembrance books listing all the names of the fallen.

The **main shrine,** featuring a green Italian-marble memorial that contains the original WWI rolls of honor, sits on an exposed chunk of the castle rock. Above you, the Archangel Michael is busy slaying a dragon. The bronze frieze accurately shows the attire of various wings of Scotland's military. The stained glass starts with Cain and Abel on the left and finishes with a celebration of peace on the right. To appreciate how important this place is, consider that Scottish soldiers died at twice the rate per capita of other British soldiers in World War I.

• *There are several other exhibits (including "Prisons of War," covering the lives of POWs held in the castle in 1781), memorials, and regimental museums in the castle. If you have seen enough, the Lang Stairs near St. Margaret's Chapel are a shortcut leading down to the Argyle Battery and the exit.*

*But there is one more important stop—the National War Museum. Backtrack down the hill toward the Redcoat Café (and the One O'Clock Gun). Just before the café head downhill to the left to the museum courtyard. (If you were in a horse-drawn carriage, you'd be thankful for the courtyard's cobblestone design—rough stones in the middle so your horse could get a grip, and smooth stones on the outside so your ride was even.) The statue in front of the museum is **Field Marshall Sir Douglas Haig**—the Scotsman who commanded the British Army through the WWI trench warfare of the Battle of the Somme and in Flanders Fields.*

🔟 **National War Museum Scotland:** This thoughtful museum covers four centuries of Scottish military history. Instead of the usual musty, dusty displays of endless armor, there's a compelling mix of videos, uniforms, weapons, medals, mementos, and eloquent excerpts from soldiers' letters. Your castle audioguide

Robert the Bruce (1274-1329)

In 1314, Robert the Bruce's men attacked Edinburgh's Royal Castle, recapturing it from the English. It was just one of many intense battles between the oppressive English and the plucky Scots during the Wars of Independence.

In this era, Scotland had to overcome not only its English foes but also its own divisiveness—and no one was more divided than Robert the Bruce. As earl of Carrick, he was born with blood ties to England and a long-standing family claim to the Scottish throne.

When England's King Edward I ("Longshanks") conquered Scotland in 1296, the Bruce family welcomed it, hoping Edward would defeat their rivals and put Bruce's father on the throne. They dutifully signed the "Ragman's Roll" of allegiance—and then Edward chose someone else as king.

Twentysomething Robert the Bruce (the "the" comes from his original family name of "de Bruce") then joined William Wallace's revolt against the English. As legend has it, he was the one who knighted Wallace after the victory at Stirling Bridge. When Wallace fell from favor, Bruce became a guardian of Scotland (caretaker ruler in the absence of a king) and continued fighting the English. But when Edward's armies again got the upper hand in 1302, Robert—along with Scotland's other nobles—diplomatically surrendered and again pledged loyalty.

In 1306, Robert the Bruce murdered his chief rival and boldly claimed to be king of Scotland. Few nobles supported him. Edward crushed the revolt and kidnapped Bruce's wife, the Church excommunicated him, and Bruce went into hiding on a distant North Sea island. He was now the king of nothing. Legend says he gained inspiration by watching a spider patiently build its web.

The following year, Bruce returned to Scotland and wove alliances with both nobles and the Church, slowly gaining acceptance as Scotland's king by a populace chafing under English rule. On June 24, 1314, he decisively defeated the English (now led by Edward's weak son, Edward II) at the Battle of Bannockburn. After a generation of turmoil (1286-1314), England was finally driven from Scotland, and the country was united under Robert I, king of Scotland.

As king, Robert the Bruce's priority was to stabilize the monarchy and establish clear lines of succession. His descendants would rule Scotland for the next 400 years, and even today, Bruce blood runs through the veins of King Charles III and his descendants.

includes coverage of this museum, and the 13-minute introductory video in the theater is worth watching.

Here you'll learn the story of how the fierce and courageous Scottish warrior changed from being a symbol of resistance against Britain to being a champion of that same empire. Along the way, these military men received many decorations for valor and did more than their share of dying in battle. But even when fighting alongside—rather than against—England, Scottish regiments still promoted their romantic, kilted-warrior image.

Queen Victoria fueled this ideal throughout the 19th century. She was infatuated with the Scottish Highlands and the culture's untamed, rustic mystique. Highland soldiers, especially officers, went to great personal expense to sport all their elaborate regalia, and the kilted men fought best to the tune of their beloved bagpipes. For centuries the stirring drone of bagpipes accompanied Highland soldiers into battle—raising their spirits and announcing to the enemy that they were about to meet a fierce and mighty foe.

This museum shows the human side of war as well as the cleverness of government-sponsored ad campaigns that kept the lads enlisting. Two centuries of recruiting posters make the same pitch that still works today: a hefty signing bonus, steady pay, and job security with the promise of a manly and adventurous life—all spiked with a mix of pride and patriotism.

Leaving the castle complex, you're surrounded by cannons that no longer fire, stony walls that tell an amazing story, dramatic views of this grand city, and the clatter of tourists (rather than soldiers) on cobbles. Consider for a moment all the bloody history and valiant struggles, along with British power and Scottish pride, that have shaped the city over which you are perched.

SIGHTS ON AND NEAR THE ROYAL MILE

For locations, see the "Royal Mile Walk" map, earlier.

▲Camera Obscura

A big deal when it was built in 1853, this observatory topped with a mirror reflected images onto a disc before the wide eyes of people who had never seen a photograph or a captured image. Today, you can climb 100 steps for an entertaining 10-minute demonstration (3/hour). At the top, enjoy the best view anywhere of the Royal Mile. This attraction is a goofy and entertaining break from all the heavy history and culture of the city's standard sights—it's just flat-out fun. On your way up and down, you'll be routed through five floors of illusions, holograms, and entertaining gags.

Cost and Hours: £19; in peak season book online a few days in advance to ensure entry and to skip the ticket-buying line; open daily July-Aug 8:00-22:00, off-season 9:00-19:00—but often until later on weekends, +44 131 226 3709, www.camera-obscura. co.uk.

▲The Scotch Whisky Experience

This attraction seems designed to distill money out of your pocket. The 50-minute experience consists of a "Malt Disney" whisky-bar-

rel ride through the production process followed by an explanation and movie about Scotland's five main whisky regions. Though gimmicky, it does succeed in providing an entertaining yet informative orientation to the creation of Scottish firewater (things get pretty psychedelic when you hit the yeast stage). Your ticket also includes sampling a wee dram and the chance to stand amid the world's largest Scotch whisky collection (almost 3,500 bottles). At the end, you'll find yourself in the bar, with a fascinating wall of unusually shaped whisky bottles. Serious connoisseurs should stick with the more substantial shops in town, but this place can be worthwhile for beginners.

Cost and Hours: £19 "silver tour" includes one sample, £30 "gold tour" includes five samples—one from each main region; generally daily 10:00-18:30, last tour at 17:30; +44 131 220 0441, www.scotchwhiskyexperience.co.uk. Here's a tip: Couples can buy one "silver" ticket and one "gold" ticket and share the samples.

▲▲Gladstone's Land

This is a typical 16th- to 17th-century merchant's "land," or tenement building. These multistory structures—in which merchants ran their shops on the ground floor and lived upstairs—were typical of the time (the word "tenement" didn't have the slum connotation then that it has today). At six stories, this one was still just half the height of the tallest "skyscrapers." Gladstone's Land comes complete with an almost-lived-in, furnished interior under 400-year-old painted ceiling beams. While this is a fascinating sight in its own right, it's made meaningful by wonderful, informative volunteers who love to tell its story—don't visit without chatting with them.

Cost and Hours: £7.50, daily 10:00-15:00—last entry time, +44 131 226 5856, www.nts.org.uk/visit/gladstones-land.

Visiting the Museum: Buy your ticket at the café counter downstairs, then head up the external staircase to go inside. Until 14:30, your entry is "self-guided"—you'll walk around on your own and learn from the docents in various rooms. Each day at 15:00, you can join a complete guided tour of the complex (no extra charge; explained on sign at entrance).

Each of the three floors has been restored to a different time period. You'll begin high up on the **third floor,** a boarding house from the 1910s. Three men would have shared this small space, with its wrought-iron beds, newspaper clippings and pinup girls stuck to the walls, and old-time records on the phonograph. The **second floor** is a drapers' shop (selling cloth, clothes, and hats) from 1766, with a work counter and a space for entertaining customers in the front, and a small back office behind. And the **first floor** is the most atmospheric, done up as the 1632 residence of an upper-middle-class trader of exotic goods. You'll see the 17th-century penchant for dark, chunky oak furniture, then head through the kitchen (with the maid's cot in the corner) to a back room that displays some of the goods that were shipped far and wide. There's also a small exhibit on the history of the building.

After visiting, keep this place in mind as you stroll the rest of the Mile, imagining other houses as if they still looked like this on the inside. (For a comparison of life in the Old Town versus the New Town, also visit the Georgian House, described later.)

▲Writers' Museum at Lady Stair's House

This aristocrat's house, built in 1622, is filled with well-described manuscripts and knickknacks of Scotland's three greatest literary figures: Robert Burns, Robert Louis Stevenson, and Sir Walter Scott. If you'd like to see Scott's pipe and Burns' snuffboxes, you'll love this little museum. You'll wind up steep staircases through a maze of rooms as you peruse first editions and keepsakes of these celebrated writers. Edinburgh's high society gathered in homes like this in the 1780s to hear the great poet Rabbie Burns read his work—it's meant to be read aloud rather than to oneself.

Cost and Hours: Free, daily 10:00-17:00, +44 131 529 4901, www.edinburghmuseums.org.uk.

Museum on the Mound

Located in the basement of the grand Bank of Scotland building, this exhibit tells the story of the bank, which was founded in 1695 (making it only a year younger than the Bank of England) and claims to be the longest operating bank in the world. Featuring lots of artifacts and displays on cash production, safe technology, and bank robberies, this museum (with a case holding £1 million in cash) makes banking almost interesting. It's worth popping in if you have extra time or find the subject appealing.

Cost and Hours: Free; Tue-Fri 10:00-17:00, Sat from 13:00, closed Sun-Mon; down Bank Street from the Royal Mile—follow the street around to the left and enter through the gate, +44 131 243 5464, www.museumonthemound.com.

▲National Library of Scotland

Just a half-block off the Royal Mile, the National Library's Treasures room hosts thought-provoking exhibits about the Scottish literary tradition, and is worth the detour for book lovers.

Cost and Hours: Free, £3 suggested donation; Mon-Thu 9:30-19:00, Fri-Sat until 17:00, closed Sun; shop and café, near George IV Bridge at 92 Cowgate, +44 131 623 3700, www.nls.uk.

Visiting the Library: To the right of the main entrance, the small Treasures collection is lovingly displayed and well described in three languages: English, Gaelic, and Scots. While displays may rotate in and out, the library's treasures include the Iona Psalter (a precious ecclesiastical book from around 1180-1220); Rabbie Burns' handwritten lyrics to his love song, "Ae Fond Kiss" (1791); and a 15th-century Gaelic manuscript about folk remedies. You may also see maps and contemporary accounts of the Jacobite Rising and battle at Culloden; tales and watercolors from Isobel Wylie Hutchison's (1889-1982) journeys to Greenland, arctic Canada, and Alaska in the 1920s and 30s; correspondence between Scottish composer George Thomson and Beethoven; elegantly bound books showing off the "wheel" and "herringbone" binding methods from 17th-century printers; and a Gutenberg bible. A nearby room hosts temporary exhibits.

▲▲St. Giles' Cathedral

This is Scotland's most important church. Its ornate spire—the Scottish crown steeple from 1495—is a proud part of Edinburgh's skyline. The fascinating interior contains nearly 200 memorials honoring distinguished Scots through the ages.

Cost and Hours: Free, £5 suggested donation; Mon-Fri 10:00-18:00, Sat 9:00-17:00, Sun 13:00-17:00; +44 131 226 0677, www.stgilescathedral.org.uk.

Concerts: St. Giles' busy concert schedule includes free organ recitals and visiting choirs (see schedule or ask for *Music at St. Giles* pamphlet at welcome desk or gift shop).

◐ Self-Guided Tour: Today's facade is 19th-century Neo-Gothic, but most of what you'll see inside is from the 14th and 15th

centuries. Engage the cathedral guides in conversation; you'll be glad you did.

As you enter, you'll begin by looping around the right side of the cathedral. Partway along this wall, above an alcove just before the organ, look for the dramatic ❶ **stained-glass window** showing the commotion

that surrounded the great reformer John Knox (1514-1572) when he preached. The bearded, fiery-eyed Knox had a huge impact on this community.

Knox, the founder of austere Scottish Presbyterianism, first preached here in 1559. His insistence that every person should be able to personally read the word of God gave Scotland an educational system 300 years ahead of the rest of Europe. Thanks partly to Knox, it was Scottish minds that led the way in math, science, medicine, and engineering. Voltaire called Scotland "the intellectual capital of Europe."

Knox preached Calvinism. Consider that the Dutch and the Scots both embraced this creed of hard work, frugality, and strict ethics. This helps explain why the Scots are so different from the English (and why the Dutch and the Scots—both famous for their thriftiness and industriousness—are so much alike).

Looking at this window, notice how there were no pews back then. The church was so packed, people even looked through clear

windows from across the street. With his hand on the holy book, Knox seems to conduct divine electricity to the Scottish faithful.

Next up, take in the sheer might of the giant ❷ **organ** (1992, Austrian-built, one of Europe's finest).

EDINBURGH

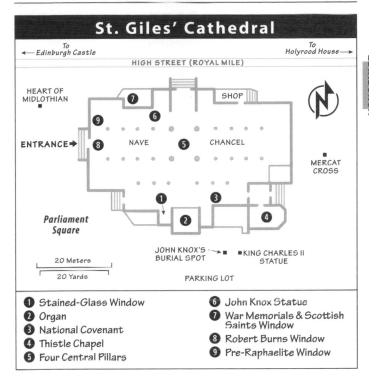

St. Giles' Cathedral

To
← Edinburgh Castle

To
Holyrood House →

HIGH STREET (ROYAL MILE)

HEART OF
MIDLOTHIAN ■

❼

SHOP

❾

❻

ENTRANCE →

❽

NAVE

❺

CHANCEL

■
MERCAT
CROSS

❶

❸

Parliament
Square

❷

❹

20 Meters

20 Yards

JOHN KNOX'S - - →■
BURIAL SPOT

■KING CHARLES II
STATUE

PARKING LOT

❶ Stained-Glass Window
❷ Organ
❸ National Covenant
❹ Thistle Chapel
❺ Four Central Pillars

❻ John Knox Statue
❼ War Memorials & Scottish Saints Window
❽ Robert Burns Window
❾ Pre-Raphaelite Window

Just past the organ, look for a glass case in a stand that holds a replica of the ❸ **National Covenant.** The original was signed in blood in 1638 by Scottish heroes who refused to compromise their religion for the king's. Most who signed were martyred (their monument is nearby, at Grassmarket). You can see the original National Covenant in the Museum of Edinburgh.

Head toward the east (back) end of the church, and turn right to find the Neo-Gothic ❹ **Thistle Chapel** (the volunteer guide here is a wealth of information). The interior is filled with intricate wood carving. Built in two years (1910-1911), entirely with Scottish materials and labor, this is the private chapel of the Order of the Thistle, the only Scottish chivalric order. It's used several times a year for the knights to gather (and, if one dies, to inaugurate a new member). Scotland recognizes its leading citizens by bestowing a membership upon them. The reigning monarch presides over the ritual from a fancy stall, marked by the Scottish coat of arms—a heraldic zoo of symbolism. Are there bagpipes in heaven? Find the tooting stone angel at the top of a window to the left of the altar, and the wooden one to the right of the doorway you came in.

Now head to the center of the nave and take it all in. Slowly walk up to the altar in the very middle of the building, surrounded by ❺ **four massive central pillars**—the oldest part of the church. These are Norman and date from the 12th century. They supported a mostly wooden superstructure that was lost when an invading English force burned it in 1385. The Scots rebuilt it bigger and better than ever, and in 1495 its famous crown spire was completed.

During the Reformation—when Knox preached here (1559-1572)—the place was simplified and whitewashed. Before this, when the emphasis was on holy services provided by priests, there were lots of little niches. With the new focus on sermons rather than rituals, the grand pulpit took center stage.

Knox preached against anything that separated you from God, including stained glass (considered the poor man's Bible, as illiterate Christians could learn from its pictures). Knox had the church's fancy medieval glass windows replaced with clear glass, but 19th-century Victorians took them out and installed the brilliantly colored ones you see today.

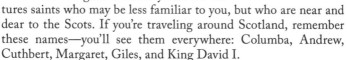

As you face the altar, head to the left side of the church. Along this north wall, look for the ❻ **John Knox's statue** (standing like a six-foot-tall bronze chess piece). Get up close. Look into his eyes for 10 seconds from 10 inches away, and think of the Reformation struggles of the 16th century.

Past Knox, the wall is lined with ❼ **war memorials.** Recalling those lost in battle is important to the Scots; every village has a monument at its main intersection listing local boys (and girls) lost in major wars. The second stained-glass window you'll see features saints who may be less familiar to you, but who are near and dear to the Scots. If you're traveling around Scotland, remember these names—you'll see them everywhere: Columba, Andrew, Cuthbert, Margaret, Giles, and King David I.

Before leaving, head back into the nave and look above the entrance toward the modern stained-glass ❽ **Robert Burns window,** which celebrates Scotland's favorite poet (see page 56). It was created in 1985 by the Icelandic artist Leifur Breiðfjörð. The green of the lower level symbolizes the natural world—God's creation. The middle zone with the circle shows the brotherhood of man—Burns was a great internationalist. The top is a rosy red sunburst of creativity, reminding Scots of Burns' famous line, "My love is like a red, red rose"—part of a song near and dear to every Scottish heart.

Finally, to the right of the Burns window is a fine ❾ **Pre-**

Raphaelite window. Like most in the church, it's a memorial to an important patron (in this case, John Marshall).

Old Parliament House

This space housed the Scottish parliament until the Act of Union in 1707. The building now holds the Scottish Supreme Court, so you'll need to go through security as you enter. Peruse the grand hall, with its fine 1639 hammer-beam ceiling and stained glass. The biggest stained-glass window depicts the initiation of the first Scottish High Court in 1532. The building is busy with wigged and robed lawyers hard at work in the old library (peek through the door) or pacing the hall deep in discussion. The basement café is literally their supreme court's restaurant (open to public until 14:30).

Cost and Hours: Free, public welcome Mon-Fri 9:00-16:30, closed Sat-Sun, no photos, enter behind St. Giles' Cathedral at door #11; open-to-the-public trials are just across the street at the High Court—the doorman has the day's docket.

▲The Real Mary King's Close

For an unusual peek at Edinburgh's gritty, plague-ridden past, join a costumed performer on an entertaining hour-long trip through an excavated underground street and buildings on the northern slope of the Royal Mile. Tours cover the standard goofy, crowd-pleasing ghost stories, but also focus on authentic and historical insight into a part of town entombed by later construction. Book ahead (online up to the day before, or by phone or in person for a same-day booking).

Cost and Hours: £19.50, book at least one day in advance during peak season; tours leave every 15-30 minutes; Mon-Fri 9:30-17:00, Sat-Sun until 21:00, these are last tour times; across from St. Giles at 2 Warriston's Close—but enter through door on High Street, +44 131 225 0672, www.realmarykingsclose.com.

▲Museum of Childhood

This five-story playground of historical toys and games is rich in nostalgia and history. Each well-signed gallery is as jovial as a Norman Rockwell painting, highlighting the delights and simplicity of childhood. The museum does a fair job of representing culturally relevant oddities, such as ancient Egyptian, Peruvian, and voodoo dolls, and displays early versions of toys it's probably best didn't make the final cut (such as a grim snake-centered precursor to the popular board game Chutes and Ladders).

Cost and Hours: Free, daily 10:00-17:00, 42 High Street, www.edinburghmuseums.org.uk.

▲John Knox House

Intriguing for Reformation buffs, this fine medieval house dates back to 1470 and offers a well-explained look at the life of the great

EDINBURGH

Scotland's Literary Greats

Edinburgh was home to Scotland's three greatest literary figures: Robert Burns, Robert Louis Stevenson, and Sir Walter Scott.

Robert Burns (1759-1796), known as "Rabbie" in Scotland and quite possibly the most famous and beloved Scot of all time, moved to Edinburgh after achieving overnight celebrity with his first volume of poetry (staying in a house on the spot where Deacon Brodie's Tavern now stands). Even though he wrote in the rough Scots dialect and dared to attack social rank, he was a favorite of Edinburgh's high society, who'd gather in fine homes to hear him recite his works.

One hundred years later, **Robert Louis Stevenson** (1850-1894) also stirred the Scottish soul with his pen. An avid traveler who always packed his notepad, Stevenson created settings that are vivid and filled with wonder. Traveling through Scotland, Europe, and around the world, he distilled his adventures into Romantic classics, including *Kidnapped* and *Treasure Island* (as well as *The Strange Case of Dr. Jekyll and Mr. Hyde*). Stevenson, who was married in San Francisco and spent his last years in the South Pacific, wrote, "Youth is the time to travel—both in mind and in body—to try the manners of different nations." He said, "I travel not to go anywhere...but to simply go." Travel was his inspiration and his success.

Sir Walter Scott (1771-1832) wrote the *Waverley* novels, including *Ivanhoe* and *Rob Roy*. He's considered the father of the Romantic historical novel. Through his writing, he generated a worldwide interest in Scotland, and reawakened his fellow coun-

16th-century reformer. Although most contend he never actually lived here, preservationists called it "Knox's house" to save it from the wrecking ball in the 1840s. Regardless, the place has good information on Knox and his intellectual sparring partner, Mary, Queen of Scots. Imagine the Protestant firebrand John Knox and the devout Catholic Mary sitting face-to-face in old rooms like these, discussing the most intimate matters of their

spiritual lives as they decided the course of Scotland's religious future. The sparsely furnished house contains some period furniture, an early 1600s hand-painted ceiling, information on the house and its resident John Mossman (goldsmith to Mary, Queen of Scots), and exhibits on printing—an essential tool for early reformers.

trymen's pride in their heritage. His novels helped revive interest in Highland culture—the Gaelic language, kilts, songs, legends, myths, the clan system—and created a national identity. An avid patriot, he wrote, "Every Scottish man has a pedigree. It is a national prerogative, as unalienable as his pride and his poverty." Scott is so revered in Edinburgh that his towering Neo-Gothic monument dominates the city center. With his favorite hound by his side, Sir Walter Scott overlooks the city that he inspired, and that inspired him.

The best way to learn about and experience these literary greats is to visit the Writers' Museum at Lady Stair's House (see page 50) and to take Edinburgh's Literary Pub Tour (see page 92).

While just three writers dominate your Edinburgh sightseeing, consider also the other great writers with Edinburgh connections: current resident Ian Rankin (with his "tartan noir" novels); J. K. Rowling (Harry Potter series); J. M. Barrie (who attended University of Edinburgh and later created Peter Pan); Sir Arthur Conan Doyle (who was born in Edinburgh, went to medical school here, and is best known for inventing Sherlock Holmes); and James Boswell (who lived 50 yards away from the Writers' Museum, in James Court, and is revered for his biography of Samuel Johnson).

Cost and Hours: £6, daily 10:00-18:00, 43 High Street, +44 131 556 9579, www.scottishstorytellingcentre.com.

▲People's Story Museum

This engaging exhibit, which occupies the Canongate Tolbooth (built in 1591), traces the working and social lives of ordinary people through the 18th, 19th, and 20th centuries (including 1970s punks and 1980s mallrats). You'll see tools, products, and objects related to important Edinburgh trades (printing, brewing), a wartime kitchen, and a small theater on the top floor with a video.

Cost and Hours: Free, daily 10:00-17:00, 163 Canongate, +44 131 529 4057, www.edinburghmuseums.org.uk.

▲Museum of Edinburgh

Another old house full of old stuff, this one is worth a stop for a look at its early Edinburgh history (and its handy ground-floor WC). Be sure to see the original copy of the National Covenant—written in 1638 on animal skin. Scottish leaders signed this, refusing to adopt the king's religion—and were killed because of it. Exploring the rest of the collection, keep an eye out for Robert Louis Stevenson's antique golf ball, James Craig's architectural plans for the Georgian New Town, an interactive kids' area with dress-up clothes, a sprawling top-floor exhibit on Edinburgh-born Field Marshall Sir David Haig (who led the British Western Front efforts in World War I and later became Earl Haig), and locally made glass and ceramics.

Cost and Hours: Free, daily 10:00-17:00, 142 Canongate, +44 131 529 4143, www.edinburghmuseums.org.uk.

Nearby: Next to the museum (uphill) is the entry to **Bakehouse Close,** a well-preserved 18th-century alleyway. It's worth a peek (and recognizable to fans of the *Outlander* TV series—the exterior of Jamie's print shop was filmed here).

▲▲Scottish Parliament Building

Scotland's parliament originated in 1293 and was dissolved when Scotland united with England in 1707. But after the Scottish electorate and the British parliament gave their consent, in 1997 it was decided that there should again be "a Scottish parliament guided by justice, wisdom, integrity, and compassion." Formally reconvened by Queen Elizabeth in 1999 (note that, while she was "II" in England, she was only the first "QE" for the people of  Scotland), the Scottish parliament now enjoys self-rule in many areas (except for matters of defense, foreign policy, immigration, and taxation). The current government, run by the Scottish Nationalist Party (SNP), is pushing for even more independence.

The innovative building, opened in 2004, brought together all the functions of the fledgling parliament in one complex. It's a people-oriented structure conceived by Catalan architect Enric Miralles. Signs are written in both English and Gaelic (the Scots' Celtic tongue).

For a peek at the building and a lesson in how the Scottish parliament works, drop in, pass through security, and find the visitors' desk. You're welcome in the public parts of the building, including a small ground-floor exhibit on the parliament's history and function and, up the stairs, a viewing gallery overlooking the impressive Debating Chambers.

Cost and Hours: Free; Mon-Sat 10:00-17:00, Tue-Thu 9:00-18:30 when parliament is in session (Sept-June), closed Sun year-round. For a complete list of recess dates or to book tickets for debates, check their website or call their visitor services line, +44 131 348 5200, www.parliament.scot.

Tours: Proud locals offer worthwhile free 45-minute **tours** covering history, architecture, parliamentary processes, and other topics. Tours generally run throughout the day Mon and Fri-Sat in session (Sept-June) and Mon-Sat in recess (July-Aug). While you can try dropping in, these tours can book up—it's best to book ahead online or over the phone.

Seeing Parliament in Session: The public can witness the Scottish parliament's hugely popular debates (usually Tue-Thu 14:00-18:00, but hours can vary). Book ahead online no more than seven days in advance, over the phone, or at the info desk. You're not required to stay the whole session.

You can also watch parliamentary committees in session (usually Tue-Thu mornings). Topics are published the Friday before (see business bulletin on website), and you must book ahead just as you would for debates.

On Thursdays from 11:40 to 12:45 the First Minister is on the hot seat and has to field questions from members across all parties (reserve ahead for this popular session over the phone a week in advance; spots book up quickly—call at 9:00 sharp on Thu for the following week). If you don't get tickets over the phone, show up at 10:00 and ask if you can get in—they sometimes have standby tickets.

▲▲Palace of Holyroodhouse

Built on the site of the abbey/monastery founded in 1128 by King David I, this palace was the true home, birthplace, and coronation spot of Scotland's Stuart kings in their heyday (James IV; Mary, Queen of Scots; and

Charles I). It's particularly memorable as the site of some dramatic moments from the short reign of Mary, Queen of Scots—including the murder of her personal secretary, David Rizzio, by agents of her jealous husband. Until her death, it was one of Queen Elizabeth II's official residences. She managed her Scottish affairs here during Holyrood Week, from late June to early July (and generally stayed at Balmoral in August). Holyrood is open to the public outside of the royal visits. Touring the interior offers a more polished contrast to Edinburgh Castle, and is particularly worth considering if you don't plan to go to Balmoral. The one-way audioguide route leads you through the fine apartments and tells some of the notable stories that played out here.

Cost: £17.50, includes quality one-hour audioguide, £23.40 combo-ticket includes the Queen's Gallery, tickets sold in Queen's Gallery to the right of the castle entrance (see next listing).

Hours: Daily 9:30-18:00, Nov-March until 16:30, last entry 1.5 hours before closing, +44 131 556 5100, www.rct.uk. It's still a working palace, so it's closed when VIPs are in residence.

Eating: The **$$$ café** on the palace grounds, to the right of the palace entrance, has an inviting afternoon tea.

Visiting the Palace: The building, rich in history and decor, is filled with elegantly furnished Victorian rooms and a few darker, older rooms with glass cases of historic bits and Scottish pieces that locals find fascinating. Bring the palace to life with the audioguide. The tour route leads you into the grassy inner courtyard, then up to the royal apartments: dining rooms, *Downton Abbey*-style drawing rooms, and royal bedchambers. Along the way, you'll learn the story behind the 96 portraits of Scottish leaders (some real, others imaginary) that line the Great Gallery; why the king never slept in his official "state bed"; and why the exiled Comte d'Artois took refuge in the palace. Finally, you'll twist up a tight spiral staircase to the private chambers of Mary, Queen of Scots, where conspirators stormed in and stabbed her secretary 56 times.

After exiting the palace, you're free to stroll through the evocative **ruined abbey** (destroyed by the English during the time of Mary, Queen of Scots, in the 16th century) and the **palace gardens** (closed Nov-March except some weekends). Some 8,000 guests—including many honored ladies sporting fancy hats—gather here every July when the royal family hosts a magnificent tea party. (They get help pouring.)

Nearby: Hikers, note that the wonderful trail up **Arthur's Seat** starts just across the street from the gardens (see page 80 for details). From the palace, face parliament, turn left, and head straight.

▲Queen's Gallery, Palace of Holyroodhouse

Over more than five centuries, the royal family has collected a wealth of art treasures. While most of the collection is kept in

the royals' many private palaces, they share an impressive sampling of it in this small museum, with themed exhibits changing about every six months. Though the gallery occupies just a few rooms, its displays can be exquisite.

Cost and Hours: £8.50 includes excellent audioguide, £23.40 combo-ticket includes Palace of Holyroodhouse; daily 9:30-18:00, Nov-March until 16:30, last entry one hour before closing; www.rct.uk. Buses #35 and #36 stop outside, saving you a walk to or from Princes Street/North Bridge.

Dynamic Earth

Located about a five-minute walk from the Palace of Holyroodhouse, this immense exhibit tells the story of our planet, filling several underground floors under a vast, white Gore-Tex tent. It's pitched, appropriately, at the base of the Salisbury Crags. The exhibit is designed for younger kids and does the same thing an American science exhibit would do—but with a charming Scottish accent. You'll learn about the Scottish geologists who pioneered the discipline, then step into a "time machine" to watch the years rewind, from cave dwellers to dinosaurs to the Big Bang. After viewing several short films on stars, tectonic plates, ice caps, and worldwide weather (in a "4-D" exhibit), you're free to wander past salty pools and a re-created rain forest.

Cost and Hours: £17.50, kids-£11; Mon-Fri 10:00-16:30, Sat-Sun until 17:30, last entry 1.5 hours before closing; on Holyrood Road, between the palace and mountain, +44 131 550 7800, www.dynamicearth.co.uk.

SIGHTS SOUTH OF THE ROYAL MILE

For locations, see the "Royal Mile Walk" map, earlier.

▲▲National Museum of Scotland

This gigantic museum has amassed more historic artifacts than every other place I've seen in Scotland combined. It's all wonderfully displayed, with fine descriptions offering an insightful and substantial hike through the history of Scotland.

Cost and Hours: Free, daily 10:00-17:00; two long blocks south of St. Giles' Cathedral and the Royal Mile, on Chambers Street off George IV Bridge, +44 131 123 6789, www.nms.ac.uk.

Tours: The museum sometimes offers free one-hour **tours** of collection highlights; ask when you arrive, or check the latest schedule online. Everything inside is well described, and interactive kiosks help navigate the stories behind important artifacts and figures.

Eating: A **$$ brasserie** is on the ground floor right next to the entrance door, and a **$ café** with coffee, tea, cakes, and snacks is on the level 3 balcony overlooking the Grand Gallery. A number of good eating options are within a couple of blocks of the museum (see page 111).

Overview: The museum can be overwhelming, so pick up the map when you enter to sort through your options: There are exhibits about natural science (T. Rex skeletons and other animals), technology, fashion, art, design, world cultures, and more.

My tour is devoted to the Scotland galleries, which lead you through Scottish history covering Roman and Viking times, Edinburgh's witch-burning craze and clan massacres, the struggle for Scottish independence, the Industrial Revolution, and right up to Scotland in the 21st century.

◎ Self-Guided Tour: From the subterranean entrance zone, head upstairs to get oriented on level 1—in the impressive glass-roofed Grand Gallery. Use your map to locate exhibits of interest.

Before diving in, head through the door in the center of the hall marked *Discoveries* to find the **millennium clock,** a 30-foot high clock with figures that move to a Bach concerto on the hour from 11:00 to 16:00. The clock has four parts (crypt, nave, belfry, and spire) and represents the turmoil of the 20th century, with a pietà at the top.

• *To reach the Scottish history wing, exit the Grand Gallery at the far right end (as you face the main part of the museum, with the big windows and busy street at your back); you'll go under the clock and past the statue of Scottish inventor James Watt.*

On the way, you'll pass through the science and technology wing. While walking through, on your left, look for a slowly revolving glass case containing **Dolly the sheep**—the world's first cloned mammal—born in Edinburgh and now preserved here.

Continue into Hawthornden Court, passing a bank of elevators, and find the door marked *Kingdom of the Scots* on the left. This is where we'll begin our sweep through Scottish history (though if you'd like to begin even earlier, you could first detour downstairs to level -1 for Scotland's prehistoric origins—geologic formation, Celts, Romans, Vikings).

Kingdom of the Scots (c. 900s-late 1600s): From its very start, Scotland was determined to be free. You're greeted with proud quotes from what's been called the Scottish Declaration of Independence—the Declaration of Arbroath, a defiant letter written to the pope in 1320. As early as the ninth century, Scotland's patron saint, Andrew (see the small wooden statue in the next room), had—according to legend—miraculously intervened to help the Picts and Scots of Scotland remain free by defeating the Angles of England. Andrew's X-shaped cross still decorates the Scottish flag today.

Enter the first room on your right, with imposing swords and other objects related to Scotland's most famous patriots—William Wallace and Robert the Bruce. Bruce's descendants, the Stuarts, went on to rule Scotland for the next 300 years. Eventually, James VI of Scotland (see his baby cradle) came to rule England as well (as King James I of England). In the middle of the room, a massive banner of the royal arms of Britain is adorned with the motto of James VI: "Blessed are the peacemakers."

In the next room, a guillotine recalls the harsh justice meted out to criminals, witches, and "Covenanters" (17th-century political activists who opposed interference of the Stuart kings in affairs of the Presbyterian Church of Scotland). Out in the larger hall, also check out the tomb (a copy) of Mary, Queen of Scots, the 16th-century Stuart monarch

who opposed the Presbyterian Church of Scotland. Educated and raised in Renaissance France, Mary brought refinement to the Scottish throne. After she was imprisoned and then executed by Elizabeth I of England in 1587, her supporters rallied each other by invoking her memory. Pendants and coins with her portrait stoked the irrepressible Scottish spirit (see display case next to tomb).

Browse the rest of level 1 to see everyday objects from that age: carved panels, cookware, and sculptures.

• *Backtrack to Hawthornden Court and head up to level 3.*

Scotland Transformed (1700s): You'll see artifacts related to Bonnie Prince Charlie and the Jacobite rebellions as well as items related to the Treaty of Union document, signed in 1707 by the Scottish parliament. This act voluntarily united Scotland with England under the single parliament of the United Kingdom. For some Scots, this move was an inevitable step in connecting to the wider world, but for others it symbolized the end of Scotland's existence.

Union with England brought stability and investment to Scotland. In this same era, the advances of the Industrial Revolution were making a big impact on Scottish life. Mechanized textile looms (on display) replaced hand craftsmanship. The huge Newcomen steam-engine water pump helped the mining industry to develop sites with tricky drainage. Nearby is a model of a coal mine (or "colliery"); coal-rich Scotland exploited this natural resource to fuel its textile factories.

How the parsimonious Scots financed these new, large-scale enterprises is explained in an exhibit on the Bank of Scotland. Powered by the Scottish work ethic and the new opportunities that came from the Industrial Revolution, the country came into relative prosperity. Education and medicine thrived. With the dawn of the modern age came leisure time, the concept of "healthful sports," and golf—a popular Scottish pastime. On display (near the back, in a small corridor behind the machinery) are some early golf balls, which date from about 1820, made of leather and stuffed with feathers.

• *Leave this hall the way you came in, and journey up to level 5.*

Industry and Empire (1800s): Turn right and do a counterclockwise spin around this floor to survey Scottish life in the 19th century. Industry had transformed the country. Highland farmers left their land to find work in Lowland factories and foundries. Modern inventions—the phonograph, the steam-powered train, the kitchen range—revolutionized everyday life. In Glasgow near

EDINBURGH

the turn of the century, architect Charles Rennie Mackintosh helped to define Scottish Art Nouveau. Scotland was at the forefront of literature (Robert Burns, Sir Walter Scott, Robert Louis Stevenson), science (Lord Kelvin, James Watt, Alexander Graham Bell...he was born here, anyway!), world exploration (John Kirk in Africa, Sir Alexander Mackenzie in Canada), and whisky production.

• *Climb the stairs to level 6.*

Scotland: A Changing Nation (1900s-present): Turn left and do a clockwise spin through this floor to bring the story to the present day. The two world wars decimated the population of this already wee nation. In addition, hundreds of thousands emigrated, especially to Canada (where one in eight Canadians has Scottish origins). Other exhibits include shipbuilding and the fishing industry; Scots in the world of entertainment (from folk singer Donovan to actor-comedian Billy Connolly); "New Scots," non-native-born Scottish citizens who are adding their story to the tapestry of this great nation; a look at devolution from the United Kingdom (1999 opening of Scotland's own parliament, the landmark 2014 referendum on Scottish independence, and Brexit—in which 51.9 percent of the greater UK voted to leave the European Union, but only 38 percent of Scots did); and a sports Hall of Fame (from tennis star Andy Murray to auto racers Jackie Stewart and Jim Clark).

• *Finish your visit on level 7, the rooftop.*

Garden Terrace: The well-described roof garden features grasses and heathers from every corner of Scotland and spectacular views of the city.

Greyfriars Bobby Statue and Greyfriars Cemetery

This famous **statue** of Edinburgh's favorite dog is across the street from the National Museum of Scotland. Every business nearby, it seems, is named for this Victorian

Skye terrier, who is reputed to have slept upon his master's grave in Greyfriars Cemetery for 14 years. The story was immortalized in a 1960s Disney flick, but recent research suggests that 19th-century businessmen bribed a stray to hang out in the cemetery to attract sightseers. If it was a ruse, it still works.

Just behind Greyfriars Bobby is the entrance to his namesake **cemetery** (open until late). Stepping through the gate, you'll see the pink-marble grave of Bobby himself. (Rather than flowers, well-wishers bring sticks to remember Bobby. Find a twig to add to the pile, and say a word of thanks to a loyal pet or two from your own life.

The well-tended cemetery is an evocative place to stroll, and a nice escape from the city's bustle. Harry Potter fans could turn it into a scavenger hunt: J. K. Rowling sketched out her saga just around the corner at The Elephant House café—and a few of the cemetery's weather-beaten headstones bear familiar names, including McGonagall and Thomas Riddell. At the far end, past a stretch of the 16th-century Flodden Wall, peek through the black iron cemetery fence to see the frilly Gothic spires of posh George Heriot's School, said to have inspired Hogwarts. And just a few short blocks to the east is a street called...Potterrow.

The cemetery just feels made for ghost walks. It's said that the tombs with iron cages over them were designed so thieves couldn't break into the grave and steal bodies to sell to the medical school across the street (which always needed cadavers). Hmmm.

Grassmarket

Once Edinburgh's site for hangings (residents rented out their windows—above the pub wryly named The Last Drop—for the view),

today Grassmarket is a people-friendly piazza. It was originally the city's garage, a depot for horses and cows (hence the name). It's rowdy here at night—a popular place for "hen dos" and "stag dos" (bachelorette and bachelor parties). In the early evening, the Literary Pub Tour departs from here (see "Nightlife in Edinburgh," later). Some good shopping streets branch off from Grassmarket; see "Shopping in Edinburgh," later, for details.

At the top of Grassmarket is the round monument to the "Covenanters." These strict 17th-century Scottish Protestants were killed for refusing to accept the king's Episcopalian prayer book. To this day, Scots celebrate their national church's emphatically democratic government. Rather than big-shot bishops (as in the Anglican or Roman Catholic Church), they have a low-key "moderator" who's elected each year.

MUSEUMS IN THE NEW TOWN

These sights are linked by my "New Town Walk" on page 30.

▲▲Scottish National Gallery

This delightful museum has Scotland's best collection of paintings—both European and Scottish. In a short visit, you can admire well-described works by Old Masters (Raphael, Rembrandt, Rubens) and Impressionists (Monet, Degas, Gauguin) and get an introduction to talented lesser-known Scottish artists who capture the outsized Scottish spirit on canvas. Although there are  no iconic masterpieces, it's a surprisingly enjoyable collection that's truly world class.

Cost and Hours: Free, daily 10:00-17:00, café downstairs, The Mound (between Princes and Market streets), +44 131 624 6200, www.nationalgalleries.org.

Eating: Downstairs you'll find the inviting **$$$ The Scottish Café Restaurant,** offering brunch all day, full meals, cakes, and afternoon tea.

Expect Changes: The museum is wrapping up an ambitious renovation, so exhibits may be in flux. On arrival, get a map to navigate to the pieces that interest you, and ask the friendly attendants for help.

Next Door: The **Royal Scottish Academy** hosts temporary art exhibits that are usually skippable. The building is connected to the Scottish National Gallery at the Gardens level (underneath the gallery) by the Weston Link building (same hours as gallery).

❷ **Self-Guided Tour:** I've selected a few great works that best represent the collection, and that you're likely to see regardless of when you visit. First up, I've covered the European masters—focusing on pieces that have ties to Scotland, or ones that are simply undisputed highlights. Then, it's Scotland's turn—with artists and paintings that you may not yet have met...but that I'd love to introduce to you.

Part 1: European Masters

The gallery's strong points include Gothic and Renaissance art; Northern (Dutch) art; and Impressionism and Post-Impressionism. I've listed works roughly chronologically.

Van der Goes, *The Trinity Altarpiece,* c. 1473-1479: For more than five centuries, these two double-sided panels have remained

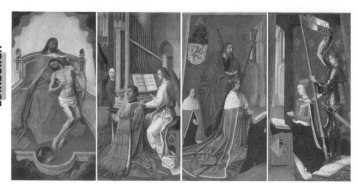

here—first in a church, then (when the church was leveled to build Waverley train station) in this museum. The panels likely were the wings of a triptych, flanking a central scene of the Virgin Mary that was destroyed by Protestant vandals during the Reformation.

In one panel is the Trinity: God the Father, in a rich red robe, cradles a spindly, just-crucified Christ, while the dove of the Holy Spirit hovers between them. (This is what would have been seen when the triptych was closed.) The flip side of the Christ panel depicts Scotland's king and queen, who are best known to history as the parents of the boy kneeling alongside them. He grew up to become James IV, the Renaissance king who made Edinburgh a cultural capital. On the other panel, the church's director (the man who commissioned the painting from the well-known Flemish painter) kneels and looks on while an angel plays a hymn on the church organ. On the opposite side is Margaret of Denmark, Queen of Scots, being presented by a saint.

In typically medieval fashion, the details are meticulous—expressive faces, intricate folds in the robes, Christ's pallid skin, observant angels. The donor's face is a remarkable portrait, with realistic skin tone and a five-o'clock shadow. But the painting lacks true 3-D realism—God's gold throne is overly exaggerated, and Christ's cardboard-cutout body hovers weightlessly.

Botticelli, *The Virgin Adoring the Sleeping Christ Child,* c. 1485: Mary looks down at her baby, peacefully sleeping in a flower-filled garden. It's easy to appreciate Botticelli's masterful style: the precisely drawn outlines, the Virgin's pristine skin, the translucent glow. Botticelli creates a serene world in which no shadows are cast. The scene is painted on canvas—unusual at a time when wood panels were the norm. For the Virgin's rich cloak, Botticelli used ground-up lapis lazuli (a very pricey semiprecious stone), and her hem is decorated with gold leaf.

Renaissance-era art lovers would instantly catch the symbolism. Mary wears a wispy halo and blue cloak that recalls the sky blue of heaven. The roses without thorns and enclosed garden are both symbols of virginity, while the violet flowers (at bottom) represent humility. Darker symbolism hints at what's to come. The strawberries (lower right) signify Christ's blood, soon to be shed, while the roses—though thornless now—will become the Crown of Thorns. For now, Mary can adore her sleeping, blissful baby in a peaceful garden. But in a few decades she'll be kneeling again to weep over the dead, crucified Messiah.

Rembrandt, *Self-Portrait,* c. 1655: It's 1655, and the middle-aged Rembrandt is on the brink of bankruptcy. Besides financial hardship and the auctioning-off of his personal belongings, he's also facing social stigma and behind-his-back ridicule. Once Holland's most renowned painter, he's begun a slow decline into poverty and obscurity.

His face says it all. Holding a steady gaze, he stares with matter-of-fact acceptance, with his lips pursed. He's dressed in dark clothes against a dark background, with the only spot of light shining on the worry lines of his forehead. Get close enough to the canvas to see the thick paste of paint he used for the wrinkles around his eyes—a study in aging.

Gainsborough, *The Honorable Mrs. Graham,* 1775-1777: The slender, elegant, lavishly dressed woman was the teenage bride of a wealthy Scottish landowner. She leans on a column, ostrich feather in hand, staring off to the side. (Thoughtfully? Determinedly? Haughtily?) Her faultless face and smooth neck stand out from the elaborately ruffled dress and background foliage. This 18th-century woman wears a silvery dress that echoes 17th-century style—Gainsborough's way of showing how, though she was young, she was classy. Thomas ("Blue Boy") Gainsborough—the product of a clothes-making father and a flower-painting mother—uses aspects of both  in this lush portrait. The ruby brooch on her bodice marks the center of this harmonious composition.

Monet, *Poplars on the River Epte,* 1891: This was part of the artist's famous "series" paintings. He set up several canvases in a floating studio near his home in Giverny. He'd start on one canvas in the morning (to catch the morning light), then move to the next as the light changed. This particular canvas captures a perfect summer day, showing both the poplars on the riverbank and their mirror image in the still water. The subject matter begins to dissolve into a pure pattern of color, anticipating abstract art.

Gauguin, *Vision of the Sermon,* 1888: Gauguin shows French peasant women imagining the miraculous event they've just heard preached about in church—when Jacob wrestles with an angel. The painting is a watershed in art history, as Gauguin throws out the rules of "realism" that had reigned since the Renaissance. The colors are surreal, there are no shadows, the figures are arranged almost randomly, and there's no attempt to make the wrestlers appear distant. The diagonal tree branch is the only thing separating the everyday world from the miraculous. Later, when Gauguin moved to Tahiti, he painted a similar world, where the everyday and magical coexist, with symbolic power.

Sargent, _Lady Agnew of Lochnaw_, 1892: This is the work that launched the career of this American-born portrait artist. Lady Agnew—the young wife of a wealthy old Scotsman—lounges back languidly and gazes out self-assuredly. The Impressionistic smudges of paint on her dress and the chair contrast with her clear skin and luminous eyeballs. Her relaxed pose (one arm hanging down the side) contrasts with her intensity: head tilted slightly down while she gazes up, a corner of her mouth askew, and an eyebrow cocked seductively.

John Emms, _Callum_, 1895: A Dandie Dinmont terrier proudly stands over a rat corpse, and looks up intently at his owner. If paintings could move, you'd see Callum's tail and little pink tongue wagging. While hardly in a league with Botticelli, Rembrandt, or Sargent, this work by the dog painter Emms has become something of a mascot for the museum. For one thing, it's cute. And for another, the dog's owner made a sizable donation to the gallery back in 1919, and one condition was that this painting must always be on display. Now that Callum has become a star, if the curators ever dared to take it down...they'd never hear the end of it.

Part 2: Scottish Artists

One of the joys of this museum is the opportunity to encounter talented Scottish artists who capture their national spirit, but who you'll rarely hear about outside of their home country. Here are a few Scottish artists and works to seek out on your visit to the museum.

Allan Ramsay (1713-1784): The son of the well-known poet of the same name painted portraits of curly-wigged men of the Enlightenment era (the philosopher David Hume, King George III) as well as likenesses of his two wives. Ramsay's portrait of the duke of Argyll—founder of the Royal Bank of Scotland—appears on the front of notes printed by that bank.

Sir Henry Raeburn (1756-1823): This portraitist chronicled the next generation, from Sir Walter Scott to the proud, kilt-wearing Alastair MacDonell. His most beloved work, *The Skating Minister,* captures Reverend Robert Walker, minister of the Canongate Church, in a moment of ice-skating reverie as he glides gracefully across the surface of Duddingston Loch.

Sir David Wilkie (1785-1841): Wilkie's forte was small-scale slices of everyday life (also called "genre scenes"). *The Letter of Introduction* (1813) captures Wilkie's own experience of trying to impress skeptical art patrons in London; even the dog is sniffing the Scotsman out. *Distraining for Rent* (1815) shows the plight of a poor farmer about to lose his farm—a common occurrence during 19th-century industrialization.

Sir Edwin Landseer (1802-1873): The aptly named Landseer was known for his Romantic depictions of the rugged Highlands. His finest work (and one of this collection's prized pieces) is *The Monarch of the Glen* (c. 1851). A 12-point stag looks nobly, even heroically, into the distance, in front of a dramatic, craggy backdrop—capturing the wild beauty of Scottish nature. You'll see other works by Landseer—which more typically juxtapose nature with humans—but this stag is iconic.

William Dyce (1806-1864): Dyce was involved in the Pre-Raphaelite movement, known for rejecting sentimental Romantic excesses and returning to medieval (that is, "Pre-Raphael") simplicity and clarity, often with bright, pure colors and a melancholy mood. *Francesca da Rimini* (1837) depicts star-crossed lovers—a young wife and her husband's kid brother—who can't help but indulge their passion. The husband later finds out and kills her; at the far left, you see his ominous hand.

William McTaggart (1835-1910): A generation younger than Landseer, McTaggart was also a landscape painter. But his work shows the influence of Impressionism—providing a glimpse of the unique light, powerful clouds, and natural wonder of the Highlands.

John Duncan (1866-1945): Duncan was a Symbolist, who depicted otherworldly scenes in pursuit of a greater truth. His intoxicating *Saint Bride* (1913) presents the story of the Celtic fifth-century saint who lived at the intersection of history and mythology. According to legend, Saint Bride was miraculously transported from the Hebrides to witness the birth of Jesus. This lyrical painting captures the fantastical scene vividly: Examine the fine details on the angels' garments and wings. Notice the seal tagging along through the churning sea under a dramatic Hebridean sky. And notice how the wings and halo break the edges of the frame-within-a-frame, creating the illusion of three dimensions.

Anne Redpath (1895-1965): Redpath was the first female painter fully admitted to the Royal Scottish Academy (in 1947) and is best known for her vivid still lifes of household objects. If you're interested in other pioneering Scottish women artists, look for portraits by **Christina Robertson** (1796-1854) and landscapes by **Josephine Haswell Miller** (1890-1975), who also taught etching and printing at the Glasgow School of Art.

▲▲Scottish National Portrait Gallery

Put a face on Scotland's history by enjoying these portraits of famous Scots from the earliest times until today. From its Neo-Gothic facade to a grand entry hall highlighting Scottish history; to galleries showcasing the great Scots of each age, this impressive museum will fascinate anyone interested in Scottish culture. The gallery also hosts temporary exhibits highlighting the work of more contemporary Scots. Because of its purely Scottish focus, many travelers prefer this to the (pan-European) main branch of the National Gallery.

Cost and Hours: Free, daily 10:00-17:00, good cafeteria serving healthy meals, 1 Queen Street, +44 131 624 6490, www.nationalgalleries.org.

Visiting the Gallery: Start by studying the gallery map and the *What's On* quarterly, which gives you a rundown of special exhibits here (and at the National Gallery and Modern Art Gallery). While the entrance hall is stirring—with a well-lit statue of poet Rabbie Burns facing all who enter, as if he's the Scottish Jesus—its history frieze up above is better viewed from the first-floor balcony (described later).

The meat of the collection is on the **top floor** (Level 2), where Scottish history is illustrated by portraits and vividly described by information plaques next to each painting. With the 20th and 21st centuries, the chronological story spills down a level into Room 12 on the first floor. The rest of the gallery is devoted to special (and often very interesting) exhibits.

• *Start on the top floor, diving right into the thick of the struggle between Scotland and England over who should rule this land.*

Reformation to Revolution (Room 1): The collection starts with a portrait of **Mary, Queen of Scots** (1542-1587), her cross and rosary prominent. This controversial ruler set off two centuries of strife. Mary was born with both Stuart blood (the ruling family of

Scotland) and the Tudor blood of England's monarchs (Queen Elizabeth I was her cousin). Catholic and French-educated, Mary felt alienated from her own increasingly Protestant homeland. Her tense conversations with the reformer John Knox must have been epic. Then came a series of scandals: She married unpopular Lord Darnley, then (possibly) cheated on him, causing Darnley to (possibly) murder her lover, causing Mary to (possibly) murder Darnley, then (possibly) run off with another man, and (possibly) plot against Queen Elizabeth.

Amid all that drama, Mary was forced by her own people to relinquish her throne to her infant son, **James VI.** Find his portraits as a child and as a grown-up. James grew up to rule Scotland, and when Queen Elizabeth (the "virgin queen") died without an heir, he also became king of England (James I). But after a bitter civil war, James' son, **Charles I,** was arrested and executed in 1649: Continuing into Room 2, see the large *Execution of Charles I* painting, his blood-dripping head displayed to the crowd. His son, Charles II, restored the Stuarts to power. He was then succeeded by his Catholic brother James VII of Scotland (II of England), who was sent into exile in France. There the Stuarts stewed, planning a return to power, waiting for someone to lead them in what would come to be known as the Jacobite rebellions.

The Jacobite Cause (a few rooms later, in Room 4): One of the biggest paintings in the room—straight ahead as you enter—is *The Baptism of Prince Charles Edward Stuart.* Born in 1720, this Stuart heir to the thrones of Great Britain and Ireland is better known to history as "Bonnie Prince Charlie." (See his bonnie features in various portraits on the wall to the left, as a child, young man, and grown man.) Charismatic Charles convinced France to invade Scotland and put him back on the throne there. In 1745, he entered Edinburgh in triumph. But he was defeated at the tide-turning Battle of Culloden (1746). The Stuart cause died forever, and Bonnie Prince Charlie went into exile, eventu-

ally dying drunk and wasted in Rome, far from the land he nearly ruled.

• *Pass through the blue Room 6, featuring the theme "Scots in Italy"— from the time when Scotland's king-in-exile, James VII/II, lived in Rome. Then move into...*

The Age of Improvement (Room 7): The faces portrayed here belonged to a new society whose hard work and public spirit achieved progress with a Scottish accent. Social equality and the Industrial Revolution "transformed" Scotland—you'll see portraits of the great poet Robert Burns, the son of a farmer (Burns was heralded as a "heaven-taught ploughman" when his poems were first published), and the man who perfected the steam engine, James Watt (on the wall to the left of Burns, upper portrait).

Heroes and Heroines (Room 8): The first part of this room celebrates female Scots from the early 20th century, including suffragette Margaret Liddell Linck; children's author and antiwar poet Lady Margaret Sackville; and opera-star-turned-wartime-nurse Mary Garden.

Linger over Cecile Walton's fascinating self-portrait *Romance*, in which the painter—clutching her baby—captures her complicated relationship with marriage, motherhood, and wealth. This work strikes a chord with its strikingly honest look at society's many expectations, and has become one of the gallery's most admired pieces.

The other half of Room 8 focuses more on male heroes: Glasgow Art Nouveau pioneer Charles Rennie Mackintosh; WWI field marshal Earl Haig; Sir James Matthew Barrie (who created *Peter Pan*); and Andrew Carnegie. There's also a portrait of a young Winston Churchill—who, despite not being Scottish, has managed to crash this gathering.

• *Finish up on this level. Room 10 features Victorian Scots, including scientist Mary Somerville and author Robert Louis Stevenson. Then head back down to the first floor for a good look at the...*

Central Atrium (first floor): Great Scots! The atrium is decorated in a parade of late-19th-century Romantic Historicism. The **frieze** (below the banister, working counterclockwise) is a visual encyclopedia, from an ax-wielding Stone Age man and a druid, to the early legendary monarchs (Macbeth), to warriors William Wallace and Robert the Bruce, to many kings (James I, II, III, and so on), to great thinkers, inventors, and artists (Allan Ramsay, Flora MacDonald, David Hume, Adam Smith, James

Boswell, James Watt), the three greatest Scottish writers (Robert Burns, Sir Walter Scott, Robert Louis Stevenson), and culminating with the historian Thomas Carlyle, who was the driving spirit (powered by the fortune of a local newspaper baron) behind creating this portrait gallery.

Around the first-floor mezzanine are large-scale **murals** depicting great events in Scottish history, including St. Columba converting the Picts (sixth century), the landing of St. Margaret at Queensferry in 1068, the Battle of Stirling Bridge in 1297, the Battle of Bannockburn in 1314, and the marriage procession of James IV and Margaret Tudor through the streets of Edinburgh in 1503.
• *Also on this floor you'll find the...*

Modern Portrait Gallery (Rooms 11-12): This space is dedicated to rotating art and photographs highlighting Scots who are making an impact in the world today, such as singer Annie Lennox, actor Alan Cumming, and physicist Peter Higgs (theorizer of the Higgs boson, the so-called God particle). Look for the *Three Oncologists,* a ghostly painting depicting the anxiety and terror of cancer and the dedication of those working so hard to conquer it.
• *And finally, also on the first floor—across the atrium—is the...*

Library: Step into this elegant old space, with two tiers of neatly stacked books and some interesting sculpture.

▲▲Georgian House

This refurbished Neoclassical house, set on Charlotte Square, is a trip back to 1796. It recounts the era when a newly gentrified and well-educated Edinburgh was nicknamed the "Athens of the North." Begin on the second floor, where you'll watch a fascinating 10-minute video dramatizing the upstairs/ downstairs lifestyles of the aristocrats and servants who lived here. Try on

some Georgian outfits, then head downstairs to tour period rooms and even peek into the fully stocked medicine cabinet. Info sheets are available in each room, along with volunteer guides who share stories and trivia, such as why Georgian bigwigs had to sit behind a screen while enjoying a fire. A walk down George Street after your visit here can be fun for the imagination.

Cost and Hours: £10; daily 10:00-17:00, shorter hours and possibly closed Nov-March, last entry one hour before closing; 7 Charlotte Square, +44 131 225 2160, www.nts.org.uk.

SIGHTS NEAR EDINBURGH
▲▲Royal Yacht *Britannia*

This much-revered vessel, which transported Britain's royal family for more than 40 years on 900 voyages (an average of once around the world per year) before being retired in 1997, is permanently moored in Edinburgh's port of Leith. The late Queen Elizabeth II said of the ship, "This is the only place I can truly relax." Today it's open to the curious public, who have access to its many decks—from engine rooms to drawing rooms—and offers a fascinating time-warp look into the late-20th-century lifestyles of the rich and royal. It's worth the 20-minute bus or taxi ride from the center; figure on spending about 2.5 hours total on the outing.

Cost and Hours: £18, includes 1.5-hour audioguide; daily 9:30-16:00, Sept-Oct from 10:00, Nov-March until 15:00, these are last-entry times; tearoom; at the Ocean Terminal Shopping Mall, on Ocean Drive in Leith; +44 131 555 5566, www.royalyachtbritannia.co.uk.

Getting There: From central Edinburgh, catch Lothian bus #11 or #16 from Princes Street (just above Waverley Station), or #35 from the National Museum or from the bottom of the Royal Mile (alongside the parliament building) to Ocean Terminal (last stop). From the B&B neighborhood south of the center, either bus to the city center and transfer to one of the buses above, or take bus #14 from Dalkeith Road to Mill Lane, then walk about 10 minutes. The Majestic Tour hop-on, hop-off bus stops here as well. If you're getting off the bus, go through the shopping center and take the escalator to level 2 (top floor).

Drivers can park free in the blue parking garage—park on level E (same floor as visitors center).

Visiting the Ship: First, explore the **museum**, filled with engrossing royal-family-afloat history. You'll see lots of family photos that evoke the fine times the Windsors enjoyed on the *Britannia,* as well as some nautical equipment and uniforms. Then, armed with your audioguide, you're welcome aboard.

This was the last in a line of royal yachts that stretches back to 1660. With all its royal functions, the ship required a crew of more than 200. Begin in the captain's bridge, which feels like it's been preserved from the day it was launched in 1953. Then head down a deck to see the officers' quarters, then the garage, where a Rolls Royce was hoisted aboard to use in places where the local transportation wasn't up to royal standards. The Veranda Deck at the back of the ship was the favorite place for outdoor entertainment. Ronald Reagan, Boris Yeltsin, Bill Clinton, and Nelson Mandela all sipped champagne here. The Sun Lounge, just off the back Veranda Deck, was the queen's favorite, with Burmese teak and the same phone system she was used to in Buckingham Palace. When she wasn't entertaining, the queen liked it quiet. The crew wore sneakers, communicated in hand signals, and (at least near the queen's quarters) had to be finished with all their work by 8:00 in the morning.

Take a peek into the adjoining his-and-hers bedrooms of Queen Elizabeth and the Duke of Edinburgh (check out the spartan twin beds), and the honeymoon suite where then-Prince Charles and Princess Di began their wedded bliss.

Heading down another deck, walk through the officers' lounge (and learn about the rowdy games they played) and past the galleys (including custom cabinetry for the fine china and silver) on your way to the biggest room on the yacht, the state dining room. Now decorated with gifts given by the ship's many noteworthy guests, this space enabled the queen to entertain a good-size  crowd. The drawing room, while rather simple (the queen specifically requested "country house comfort"), was perfect for casual relaxing among royals. Princess Diana played the piano, which is bolted to the deck. Note the contrast to the decidedly less plush crew's quarters, mail room, sick bay, laundry, and engine room.

▲Rosslyn Chapel

This small but fascinating countryside church, about a 20-minute drive outside Edinburgh, is a riot of carved iconography. The patterned ceiling and walls have left scholars guessing about the symbolism for centuries.

Cost and Hours: £9.50, Mon-Sat 9:30-17:00, Sun 12:00-16:45, located in Roslin Village, +44 131 440 2159, www.rosslynchapel.com.

Getting There: Ride Lothian bus #37 from Princes Street (stop PJ), North Bridge, or Newington Road in the B&B neighborhood (1-2/hour, 45 minutes). By car, take the A-701 to Peni-cuik/Peebles, and follow signs for *Roslin;* once you're in the village, you'll see signs for the chapel.

Background: Founded in 1446 as the private mausoleum of the St. Clair family—who wanted to be buried close to God—the church's interior is carved with a stunning mishmash of Christian, pagan, family, Templar, Masonic, and other symbolism. After the Scottish Reformation, Catholic churches like this fell into disre-pair. But in the 18th and 19th centuries, Romantics such as Robert Burns and Sir Walter Scott discovered these evocative old ruins, putting Rosslyn Chapel back on the map. Even Queen Victoria vis-ited, and gently suggested that the chapel be restored to its original state. Today, after more than a century of refits and refurbishments, the chapel transports visitors back to a distant and mysterious age. Some readers will recognize the Rosylyn Chapel for its prominent role in Dan Brown's 2003 bestseller *The Da Vinci Code.* That fame has passed but the chapel's allure endures.

Visiting the Chapel: From the ticket desk and visitors center, head to the chapel itself. Ask about docent lectures. If you have time to kill, pick up the good laminated descriptions for a clock-wise tour of the carvings. In the crypt—where the stonemasons worked—you can see faint architectural drawings engraved in the wall, used to help them plot out their master design.

Elsewhere, look for these fun details: In the corner to the left of the altar, find the angels playing instruments—including one with bagpipes. Nearby, you'll see a person dancing with a skeleton. This "dance of death" theme—common in the Middle Ages—is a reminder of mortality: We'll all die eventually, so we might as well whoop it up while we're here. On the other side of the nave are carvings of the seven deadly sins and the seven acts of mercy. One inscription reads: "Wine is strong. Kings are stronger. Women are stronger still. But truth conquers all."

Flanking the altar are two carved columns that come with a legend: The more standard-issue column, on the left, was executed by a master mason, who soon after (perhaps disappointed in his lack of originality) went on a sabbatical to gain inspiration. While he was gone, his ambitious apprentice carved the beautiful cork-screw-shaped column on the right. Upon returning, the master flew into an envious rage and murdered the apprentice with his carving hammer.

Scattered throughout the church, you'll also see the family's symbol, the "engrailed cross" (with serrated edges). Keep an eye out for the more than one hundred "green men"—chubby faces with leaves and vines growing out of their orifices, symbolizing nature. This paradise/Garden of Eden theme is enhanced by a smatter-ing of exotic animals (monkey, elephant, camel, dragon, and a lion fighting a unicorn) and some exotic foliage: aloe vera, trillium, and corn. That last one (framing a window to the right of the altar) is a mystery: It was carved well before Columbus sailed the ocean blue, at a time when corn was unknown in Europe. Several theories have been suggested—some far-fetched (the father of the man who built the chapel explored the New World before Columbus), and others more plausible (the St. Clairs were of Norse descent, and the Vikings are known to have traveled to the Americas well before Columbus). Others simply say it's not corn at all—it's stalks of wheat. After all these centuries, Rosslyn Chapel's mysteries still inspire the imaginations of historians, novelists, and tourists alike.

Royal Botanic Garden

Britain's second-oldest botanical garden (after Oxford) was established in 1670 for medicinal herbs, and this 70-acre refuge is now one of Europe's best. A visitors center has temporary exhibits. The vintage "glasshouses" (greenhouses) are being restored and will eventually reopen with paid admission.

Cost and Hours: Free; daily 10:00-18:00, Feb and Oct until 17:00, Nov-Jan until 16:00, last entry 45 minutes before closing; café and restaurant, a mile north of the city center at Inverleith Row, +44 131 248 2909, www.rbge.org.uk.

Getting There: It's a 10-minute bus ride from the city center: Take bus #8 from North Bridge, or #23 or #27 from George IV Bridge (near the National Museum) or The Mound. The Majestic Tour hop-on, hop-off bus also stops here. Or you can walk here, from Dean Village near the West End, by way of the lovely Water of Leith Walkway (see page 82).

Scottish National Gallery of Modern Art

This museum, with two buildings set in a beautiful parkland, houses Scottish and international paintings and sculpture from 1900 to the present, including works by Matisse, Duchamp, Picasso, and Warhol. The grounds include a pleasant outdoor sculpture park and a café.

Cost and Hours: Free, daily 10:00-17:00, 75 Belford Road, +44 131 624 6200, www.nationalgalleries.org.

Getting There: It's about a 20-minute walk west from the city center.

Craigmillar Castle

On the southern outskirts of Edinburgh—near the B&B neighborhood—atop a flat, grassy hill sits the fortified country residence of the Prestons of Craigmillar. While the castle is essentially an empty shell (with no significant artifacts or exhibits, aside from some good posted descriptions), it's pretty, and the top level offers distant views over Edinburgh. Kids (and kids-at-heart) enjoy

EDINBURGH

clambering around through its dark passages and halls. In the central, fortified Tower House (from 1374), you'll see the room where an ailing Mary, Queen of Scots recovered from an illness; while she was here, a plan was hatched to assassinate her husband, Lord Darnly (known to Scottish history buffs as "The Craigmillar Bond"). *Outlander* fans might recognize this place as the filming location for fictional Ardsmuir Prison. While not worth a special trip, those staying in the neighborhood might enjoy a quick stop here.

Cost and Hours: £7; daily 10:00-17:00, Oct-March until 16:00; £2.50 guidebooklet, free parking, Craigmillar Castle Road, +44 131 661 4445.

Experiences in Edinburgh

URBAN HIKES

▲▲Holyrood Park: Arthur's Seat and the Salisbury Crags

Rising up from the heart of Edinburgh, Holyrood Park is a lush green mountain squeezed between the parliament/Holyroodhouse (at the bottom of the Royal Mile) and my recommended B&B neighborhood south of the center. You can connect these two zones via an early-morning or late-evening hike (in June, the sun comes up early, and it stays light until nearly midnight). Or, for a more serious climb, make the ascent to the summit of Ar-  thur's Seat, the 822-foot-tall remains of an extinct volcano. You can run up like they did in *Chariots of Fire*, or just stroll. At the summit, you'll be rewarded with commanding views of the town and surroundings.

Hiking along the Salisbury Crags: There are three ways to connect the Royal Mile and the B&B neighborhood to the south by foot. Unfortunately, the most scenic option (called the "Radical Road" along the Salisbury Crags) has been closed for a few years due to rock falls. There are plans to reinforce the rocks and reopen the path, so ask. The other alternatives are harder (hiking steeply up along the top of those cliffs), or easier but less scenic (walking across the meadow that fills the saddle of this promontory).

From the Royal Mile: Begin in the parking lot below the Palace of Holyroodhouse. Facing the cliff, you'll see two trailheads. If the trail to the right—the "Radical Road" along the base of the Salisbury Crags—is open, take it. At the far end, you can descend into the Dalkeith Road area or continue steeply up the switchback trail to the Arthur's Seat summit (described later). If that trail is closed, head to the left (with the big playing field on your left) and find the trail that cuts through the meadow across the saddle of land between the peaks. Alternatively, you can hike steeply up to the top of the Salisbury Crags for a more demanding, but scenic, hike. These trails meet up on the other side, near the base of the Arthur's Seat hike.

From the B&B Neighborhood South of the Center: From the Commonwealth Pool, take Holyrood Park Road, bear left at the first roundabout, then turn right at the second roundabout (onto Queen's Drive). Soon you'll see the trailhead, which splits into various options. If the "Radical Road" to the left—under the dramatic cliffs—is open, take it for fantastic views as you curl  around toward the Royal Mile. Otherwise, head straight ahead across the meadow. (Or, for more of a hike, angle up to the left here to find a trail that goes along the top of the Salisbury Crags.) The steep "Piper's Walk" up to Arthur's Seat also beings here, on the right.

Summiting Arthur's Seat: For a moderately strenuous hike to a hilltop viewpoint, right in the city center, consider summiting Arthur's Seat. While the distance is not great, the hike is steep and the footing can be challenging, with irregularly spaced stone steps most of the way; as these have been worn smooth by hikers, they can be slippery on the way down, even when dry (and treacherous when wet). Those in great shape can make it from the park at the bottom to the summit in about 20 minutes; mere mortals should allow more time. The payoff at the top is sweeping, 360-degree views over all of Edinburgh and its surroundings.

The most direct route to the summit is the steep stone steps nicknamed the "Piper's Walk" that rise straight up from above the B&B neighborhood side of the hill. For a more gradual approach, curl around the back of Arthur's Seat (as you approach from the B&B area, hook around to the right). This 2.5-mile walk takes you scenically over Duddingston Loch (and Duddingston village, described later—for a longer hike, you can combine this walk with that one). When you reach the smaller lake called Dunsapie Loch, head up (either through the steep meadow or along the nearby trail) to reach the craggy top of Arthur's Seat. (Taxis can take you as far up as the Dunsapie Loch car park—trimming the walk about in half—but you still face a steep ascent from here.) Regardless of how you approach, you'll still have to traverse the final, steep, rocky path to the summit, where intrepid hikers appreciate the grand views while taking turns snapping selfies at the block marking the highest point in Edinburgh.

▲Dean Village and the Water of Leith Walkway

The Water of Leith Walkway is a 12-mile, mostly level urban trail that follows Edinburgh's river all the way to its historic port, at Leith. To escape the city on a refreshing, easy-to-follow stroll, you can follow just a short segment of the entire path. Locals enjoy the one-mile stretch from Roseburn to Dean Village, but the most popular option is to begin in Dean and walk a mile to Stockbridge, or to extend another half-mile or so to Canonmills near the Royal Botanic Garden (described below). For some light commentary en route, download free audio tour tracks at www.waterofleith.org.uk/walkway. Along the way, watch for a series of human-sized sculptures standing in the river, by British artist Antony Gormley (best known for the gigantic, winged *Angel of the North* statue you may have passed if you drove up here from England).

Beginning in Dean Village: Descend to the adorable Dean Village—situated along a bend in the river just along the northern edge of the West End. (It's an easy walk from the New Town, and reachable by several buses—including #19, #37, #41, and #43.) With the lovely river gushing through its middle, Dean has two scenic bridges, a variety of higgledy-piggledy houses, and a gigantic red-brick social housing complex from 1884 with turrets and crenellations, giving it a certain Hogwarts air. Go on a little loop through Dean, crossing both the bigger stone bridge and the lower footbridge. While it seems cute as a pin today, Dean originated as a gritty industrial slum, with churning mills and waterwheels.

Dean Village to Stockbridge and the Royal Botanic Garden: To enjoy a short stretch of the walkway, leave Dean Village at the end near the stone bridge and follow the clearly marked brown *Water of Leith Walkway* signs along "Miller Row." You'll pass under a gigantic bridge (built by Thomas Telford in 1830), then an elegant Neoclassical structure housing St. Bernard's Well. Soon you'll reach Stockbridge. Pass under the first bridge, then—at the second bridge—cross over the river to find the trail that continues along the left bank. Stockbridge is an enjoyable place to poke around, with several restaurants, cafés, pubs, and the popular Golden Hare Books.

From Stockbridge, carry on, carefully tracking *Water of Leith Walkway* signs to stay on course. You'll wind up on the thickly wooded Rocheid Path (named for the main donors of the Royal Botanic Garden) until you emerge again at a busy urban intersection called **Canonmills.** This is a good place to head up the road to enter the Royal Botanic Garden.

To Leith Through St. Mark's Park: From here you could instead continue a couple more miles all the way into Leith. Along the way, you'll pass through the beautiful St. Mark's Park, with wide, grassy lawns. As you approach Leith, the trail carries on through a little greenbelt surrounded by urban blight—less romantic, but still apart from the bustle of the city. Finally, you reach the place where the river meet the industrial basins of Leith.

Duddingston Village and Dr. Neil's Garden

This low-key, 30-minute walk goes from the B&B neighborhood south of the center to Duddingston Village—a former village that got absorbed by Edinburgh but still retains its old, cobbled feel, local church, and great old-time pub, the recommended Sheep Heid Inn. Also here is Dr. Neil's Garden, a peaceful, free garden on a loch.

Walk behind the Commonwealth Pool along Holyrood Park Road. Before the roundabout, just after passing through the wall/gate, take the path to your right. This path runs alongside the Duddingston Low Road all the way to the village and garden. Ignore the road traffic and enjoy the views of Arthur's Seat, the golf course, and eventually, Duddingston Loch. When you reach the cobbled road, you're in Duddingston Village, with the church on your right and the Sheep Heid Inn a block down on your left. Another 100 feet down the main road is a gate labeled *"The Manse"* with the number 5—enter here for the garden.

Dr. Neil's Garden (also known as the Secret Garden) was started by doctors Nancy and Andrew Neil, who traveled throughout Europe in the 1960s gathering trees and plants. They brought them back here, planted them on this land, and tended to them with the help of their patients. Today it offers a quiet, secluded break from the city, where you can walk among flowers and trees and over quaint bridges, get inspired by quotes written on chalkboards, or sit on a bench overlooking the loch (free, daily 10:00-dusk, charming café, +44 784 918 7995, www.drneilsgarden.co.uk).

▲Calton Hill

For an easy walk for fine views over all of Edinburgh and beyond, head up to Calton Hill—the monument-studded bluff that rises from the eastern end of the New Town. From the Waverley Station area, simply head east on Princes Street (which becomes Waterloo Place).

About five minutes after passing North Bridge, watch on the right for the gated entrance to the **Old Calton Cemetery**—worth a quick walk-through for its stirring monuments to great Scots. The can't-miss-it round monument honors the philosopher David

Hume; just next to that is a memorial topped by Abraham Lincoln, honoring Scottish-American troops who were killed in combat. The obelisk honors political martyrs.

The views from the cemetery are good, but for even better ones, head back out to the main road and continue a few more minutes on Waterloo Place. Across the street, steps lead up into **Calton Hill.** Explore the park, purchased by the city in 1724 and one of the first public parks in Britain. Informational plaques identify the key landmarks. At the summit of the hill is the giant, unfinished replica of the Parthenon, honoring those

lost in the Napoleonic Wars. Donations to finish it never materialized, leaving it with the nickname "Edinburgh's Disgrace." Nearby, the old observatory holds an old telescope, and the back of the hillside boasts sweeping views over the Firth of Forth and Edinburgh's sprawl. Back toward the Old Town, the tallest tower (shaped like a 19th-century admiral's telescope) celebrates Admiral Horatio Nelson—the same honoree of the giant pillar on London's Trafalgar Square. There's an interesting, free exhibit about Nelson at the base of the tower. While you can pay to climb it for the view, it doesn't gain you much. The best views are around the smaller, circular Dugald Stewart Monument, with postcard panoramas overlooking the spires of the Old Town and the New Town.

WHISKY AND GIN TASTING
Whisky Tasting
One of the most accessible places to learn about whisky is at the **Scotch Whisky Experience** on the Royal Mile, an expensive but informative overview to whisky, including a tasting (see page 49). To get more into sampling whisky, try one of the early-evening tastings at the recommended **Cadenhead's Whisky Shop** (see page 89).

The **Scotch Malt Whisky Society,** in the New Town, is for more serious whisky fans. It serves glasses from numbered bottles of single malts from across Scotland and beyond. Each bottle—pure from the cask and not blended—is only described and not labeled. You read the description and make your choice...or enlist the help of the bartender, who will probe you on what kind of flavor profile you like. While this place's shrouded-in-mystery pretense could get lost on novices, aficionados enjoy it (Tue-Sat 11:00-23:00, Sun 12:00-21:00, closed Mon; tasting events listed on website—most are around £25-40, bar serves light dishes, on-site restaurant, 28 Queen Street, +44 131 220 2044, www.smws.com).

Gin Distillery Tours

The residents of Edinburgh drink more gin per person than any other city in the United Kingdom. The city is largely responsible for the recent renaissance of this drink, so it's only appropriate that you visit a gin distillery while in town. Two distilleries right in the heart of Edinburgh offer hour-long tours with colorful guides who discuss the history of gin, show you the stills involved in the production process, and ply you with libations. Both tours are popular and fill up; book ahead on their websites.

Pickering's is located in a former vet school and animal hospital at Summerhall, halfway between the Royal Mile and the B&B neighborhood. The bar and funky distillery have a cool, young, artsy vibe with skeletons and X-rays still hanging around. The mellow bar also serves cheap pub grub (£25 includes welcome gin and tonic, tour, and 4 samples; 4/day Thu-Sun, meet at the Royal Dick Bar in the central courtyard at 1 Summerhall—for location see the map on page 104, +44 131 290 2901, www.pickeringsgin.com).

Edinburgh Gin is a showroom (not a distillery) in the West End, near the Waldorf Astoria Hotel (£25 one hour tasting includes 5 tastes, book ahead on their website; 1A Rutland Place, enter off Shandwick Place next to the Ghillie Dhu bar—for location see the map on page 101, +44 131 656 2810, www.edinburghgin. com). Even if you don't join one of their tours, you can still visit their Heads & Tales bar to taste their gins (Thu-Sat 17:00-24:00, closed Sun-Wed).

LEISURE ACTIVITIES

Several enjoyable activities cluster near the B&B area around Dalkeith Road. For details, check their websites.

The **Royal Commonwealth Pool** is an indoor fitness and activity complex with a 50-meter pool, gym/fitness studio, and kids' soft play zone (21 Dalkeith Road—see map on page 104, +44 131 667 7211, www.edinburghleisure.co.uk).

The **Prestonfield Golf Club,** also an easy walk from the B&Bs, has golfers feeling like they're in a country estate (dress code, 6 Priestfield Road North—see map on page 104, general +44 131 667 9665, reservation +44 131 667 8597, www.prestonfieldgolf. co.uk).

At the **Midlothian Snowsports Centre** (a little south of town in Hillend; better for drivers), you can try skiing without any pesky snow. It feels like snow-skiing on a slushy day, even though you're schussing over matting misted with water. Four tubing runs offer fun even for nonskiers (£15/first hour, £8/hour after that, includes gear, generally Mon-Fri 9:30-21:00, Sat-Sun until 19:00, shorter hours off-season, Biggar Road—see map on page 6, +44 131 445 4433, www.midlothian.gov.uk).

EDINBURGH'S FESTIVALS

Every summer, Edinburgh's annual festivals turn the city into a carnival of the arts. The season begins in June with the international film festival (www. edfilmfest.org.uk); then the jazz and blues festival in July (www. edinburghjazzfestival.com).

In August a riot of overlapping festivals known collectively as the **Edinburgh Festival** rages simultaneously—international, fringe, book, and art, as well as the Military Tattoo. There are enough music, dance, drama, and multicultural events to make even the most jaded traveler giddy with excitement. Every day is jammed with formal and spontaneous fun. Many city sights run on extended hours. It's a glorious time to be in Edinburgh...*if* you have (and can afford) a room.

If you'll be in town in August, book your room and tickets for major events (especially the Tattoo) as far ahead as you can lock in dates. Plan carefully to ensure you'll have time for festival activities as well as sightseeing. Check online to confirm dates; the best overall website is www.edinburghfestivalcity.com. Several publications—including the festival's official schedule, the *Edinburgh Festivals Guide Daily, The List, Fringe Program,* and *Daily Diary*—list and evaluate festival events. The *Scotsman* newspaper reviews every show.

The official, more formal **Edinburgh International Festival** is the original. Major events sell out well in advance (ticket office at the Hub, in the former Tolbooth Church near the top of the Royal Mile, +44 131 473 2000, www.eif.co.uk).

The less formal **Fringe Festival,** featuring edgy comedy and theater, is huge—with 2,000 shows—and has eclipsed the original festival in popularity (ticket/info office just below St. Giles' Cathedral on the Royal Mile, 180 High Street, bookings +44 131 226 0000, www.edfringe.com). Tickets may be available at the door, and half-price tickets for some events are sold on the day of the show at the Half-Price Hut, located at The Mound, near the Scottish National Gallery.

The **Military Tattoo** is a massing of bands, drums, and bagpipes, with groups from all over the former British Empire and beyond. Displaying military finesse with a stirring lone-piper finale, this grand spectacle fills the castle esplanade (nightly during most of Aug except Sun, performances Mon-Fri at 21:00, Sat at 18:15 and 21:30; tickets start at £30 and can get very pricey, booking starts in Dec, Fri-Sat shows sell out first, all seats generally sold out by early summer, some scattered same-day tickets may be available; office open Mon-Fri 10:00-16:30, closed Sat-Sun, during Tattoo open until show time and closed Sun; 1 Cockburn Street, behind Waverley Station, +44 131 225 1188, www.edintattoo.co.uk). Some performances are filmed by the BBC and later broadcast as a big national television special. This broadcast has become an annual ritual for the people of Britain.

Other **summer festivals** cover books (mid-late Aug, www.edbookfest.co.uk) and art (late July-Aug, www.edinburghartfestival.com). The **Festival of Politics** is held in October in the Scottish parliament building. It's a busy weekend of discussions and lectures on environmentalism, globalization, terrorism, gender, and other issues (www.festivalofpolitics.scot).

Shopping in Edinburgh

Edinburgh is bursting with Scottish clichés for sale: kilts, shortbread, whisky...if they can slap a tartan on it, they'll sell it. Locals dismiss the touristy trinket shops, which are most concentrated along the Royal Mile, as "tartan tat." Your challenge is finding something a wee bit more authentic. If you want to be sure you are taking home local merchandise, check if the label reads: "Made in Scotland." "Designed in Scotland" actually means "Made in China." Shops are usually open around 10:00-18:00 (often later on Thu, shorter hours or closed on Sun). Tourist shops are open longer hours.

SHOPPING STREETS AND NEIGHBORHOODS

Near the Royal Mile: The Royal Mile is intensely touristy, mostly lined with interchangeable shops selling made-in-China souvenirs. I've listed a few worthwhile spots along here later, under "What to Shop For." But in general, the area near Grassmarket, an easy stroll from the top of the Royal Mile, offers more originality. **Victoria Street,** which climbs steeply downhill from the Royal Mile (near the Hub/Tolbooth Church) to Grassmarket, has a fine concentration of local chain shops, including I.J. Mellis Cheesemonger and Walker Slater for designer tweed, plus a Harry Potter store, and more clothing and accessory shops. On **Grassmarket,** the Hawico shop sells top-quality cashmere milled in southern Scotland. Exiting Grassmarket opposite Victoria Street, **Candlemaker Row** is more artisan, with boutiques selling hats (from dapper men's caps to outrageous fascinators), jewelry, art, design items, and even fos-

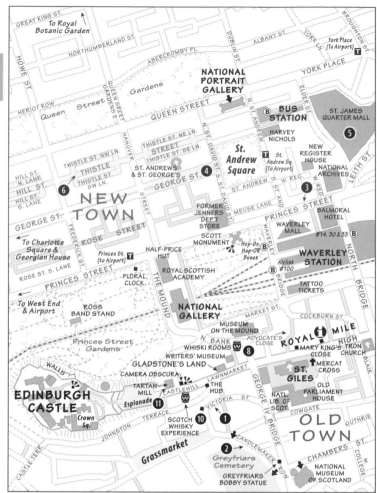

sils. The street winds a couple of blocks up toward the National Museum; Greyfriars Bobby awaits you at the top of the street.

In the New Town: For mass-market shopping, you'll find plenty of big chain stores along **Princes Street**—Marks & Spencer, H&M, Zara, Primark, and a glitzy Apple Store, and so on. Parallel to Princes Street, **George Street** has a few higher-end chain stores (including some from London, such as Molton Brown). Just off St. Andrew Square is a branch of the posh London department store Harvey Nichols. And just beyond that is the high-end **St. James Quarter** shopping mall.

For more local, artisan shopping, check out **Thistle Street,** lined with some fun eateries and a few interesting shops. You'll see some fun boutiques selling jewelry, shoes, and clothing.

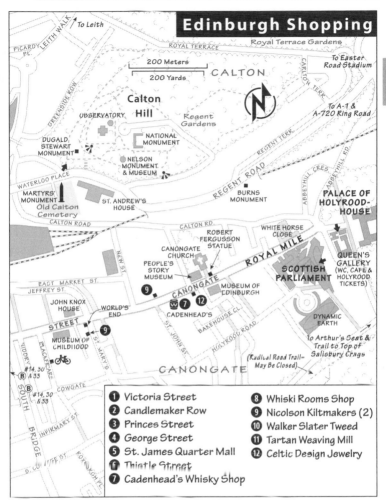

Edinburgh Shopping

1 Victoria Street
2 Candlemaker Row
3 Princes Street
4 George Street
5 St. James Quarter Mall
6 Thistle Street
7 Cadenhead's Whisky Shop
8 Whiski Rooms Shop
9 Nicolson Kiltmakers (2)
10 Walker Slater Tweed
11 Tartan Weaving Mill
12 Celtic Design Jewelry

WHAT TO SHOP FOR
Whisky

You can order whisky in just about any bar in town, and whisky shops are a dime a dozen around the Royal Mile. But the places I've listed here distinguish themselves by their tradition and helpful staff.

Cadenhead's Whisky Shop is not a tourist sight—don't expect free samples or a hand-holding shopping experience. Founded in 1842, this firm prides itself on bottling good whisky straight from casks at the distilleries, without all the compromises that come with profitable mass production (coloring with sugar to fit the expected look, watering down to reduce the alcohol tax, and so on). Those drinking from Cadenhead-bottled whiskies will enjoy the pure product as the distilleries' owners themselves do, not as the sorry public does. If you're serious about buying, the staff can explain the sometimes-complex whisky board

and talk you through flavor profiles (prices start around £8.50 for about 3.5 ounces; open Mon-Sat 10:30-17:30, closed Sun; 172 Canongate, +44 131 556 5864, www.cadenhead.scot).

Whiski Rooms Shop, just off the Royal Mile, comes with a knowledgeable, friendly staff that happily assists novices and experts alike to select the right bottle. Their adjacent bar usually has about 400 open bottles: Serious purchasers can get a sample. You can order a shareable flight in the bar, which comes with written information about each whisky you're sampling (variety of options around £28-40, available anytime the bar is open). Or you can opt for a guided tasting (£30 for one-hour introductory tasting, £50 for 1.5-hour premium tasting, chocolate and cheese pairings also available, reserve ahead; shop open daily 10:00-18:00, until 20:00 in summer, bar until 24:00; 4 North Bank Street, +44 131 225 1532, www.whiskirooms.co.uk).

Near the B&B Neighborhood: Perhaps the most accessible place to learn about local whiskies is conveniently located in the B&B area south of the city center. **Wood-Winters** has a passion both for traditional spirits and for the latest innovations in Edinburgh's booze scene. It's well stocked with 300 whiskies and gins (a trendy alternative to Scotch), as well as wines and local craft beers. Curious browsers can ask to sample a wee dram (Mon-Sat 10:00-19:00, closed Sun, 91 Newington Road—for location, see the map on page 104, +44 131 667 2760, www.woodwinters.com).

Kilts

Many of the kilt outfitters you'll see along the Royal Mile are selling cheap knockoffs, made with printed rather than woven tartan material. If you want a serious kilt—or would enjoy window-shopping for one—try the place below. These have a few off-the-rack options, but to get a kilt in your specific tartan and size, they'll probably take your measurements, custom-make it, and ship it to you. For a good-quality outfit (kilt, jacket, and accessories), plan on spending about £1,000.

Nicolson Kiltmakers has a respect for tradition and quality. Owner Gordon enlists and trains local craftspeople who specialize

in traditionally manufactured kilts and accessories. He prides himself on keeping the old ways alive (in the face of deeply discounted "tartan tat") and actively cultivates the next generation of kiltmakers (Mon-Sat 9:30-17:30, Sun 12:00-16:00, 189 Canongate, +44 131 558 2887, www.nicolsonkiltmakers.com). Their second branch, a couple of blocks up the Royal Mile at 19 St. Mary's, has rental kilts and their workshop.

Tweed

Several places around town sell the famous Harris Tweed, the authentic stuff hand woven on the Isle of Harris in the far west of

Scotland. Harris Tweed is a protected name, so if the label says "Harris," you know it's the real thing. **Walker Slater** is the place to go for top-quality tweed at top prices. They have three locations on Victoria Street, just below the Royal Mile near Grass-

market: menswear (at #16), womenswear (#44), and a sale shop (#5). You'll find a rich interior and a wide variety of gorgeous jackets, scarves, bags, and more. This place feels elegant and exclusive (Mon-Sat 10:00-18:00, Sun 11:00-17:00, www.walkerslater.com). Harris Tweed is also available at the **Tartan Weaving Mill** at the top of the Royal Mile (daily 9:00-17:30, 555 Castlehill, +44 131 220 2477).

Jewelry

Jewelry with Celtic designs, mostly made from sterling silver, is a popular and affordable souvenir. While you'll see it sold around town, **Celtic Design** (156 Canongate) offers a quality and tasteful selection.

Nightlife in Edinburgh

Night Walks

A guided evening walk is a worthwhile way to spend an evening. Here are two options.

▲▲Literary Pub Tour

This two-hour walk is interesting and a worthwhile way to spend an evening—even if you can't stand "Auld Lang Syne." Think of it as a walking theatrical performance, where you follow the witty dialogue of two actors as they debate the great literature of Scotland. (You may ask yourself if this is high art or the creative re-creation of fun-loving louts fueled by a passion for whisky.) You'll cover a lot of ground, wandering from Grassmarket over the Old Town and New Town, with stops in three to four pubs, as your guides share their takes on Scotland's literary greats. The tour meets at the Beehive Inn on Grassmarket (£20, just show up or book online and save £3, drinks extra; June-July and Sept nightly at 19:30; April-May, Aug, and Oct Thu-Sun; March and Nov-Dec Fri and Sun; Jan-Feb by request; 18 Grassmarket, +44 800 169 7410, www.edinburghliterarypubtour.co.uk).

▲Ghost Walks

A variety of companies lead spooky walks around town, providing an entertaining and affordable night out (offered nightly, most around 19:00 and 21:00, easy socializing for solo travelers). These two options are the most established.

Auld Reekie Tours offers a scary array of walks daily and nightly. Auld Reekie intertwines the grim and gory aspects of Scotland's history with the paranormal, witch covens, and pagan temples. They take groups into the "haunted vaults" under the old bridges "where it was so dark, so crowded, and so squalid that the people there knew each other not by how they looked, but by how they sounded, felt, and smelt." The guides are passionate, and the stories are genuinely spooky. Even if you don't believe in ghosts, you'll be entertained (£14-18, 1-1.5 hours, all tours leave from the tourist information kiosk in front of the modern Bank of Scotland building on the Royal Mile, opposite Deacon Brodie's Tavern at 300 Lawnmarket, +44 131 557 4700, www.auldreekietours.com).

Cadies & Witchery Tours are theatrical, with a balance of historical context and slapstick humor that's fun for families. They offer two different walks: an afternoon tour of Greyfriars Cemetery, with a bit more of a historical focus (£15, at 14:00, 1.5 hours, meet at the Cadies and Witchery Tours Shop at 84 West Bow—where Victoria Street bends down toward Grassmarket); and an evening "Ghosts and Gore" walk by a costumed guide—a bit goofier, with more jumps and scares (£13, at 19:00, 1.25 hours, leaves from outside the Witchery Restaurant at the top of Royal Mile near the Esplanade). Tours may not run every day—check schedule and make required reservations online (+44 131 225 6745, www. witcherytours.com).

Dance and Theater
Scottish Folk Dancing

Scottish variety shows include a traditional dinner with all the edible clichés, followed by a full slate of swirling kilts, blaring bagpipes, storytelling, and Scottish folk dancing. As these are designed for tour groups, you'll sit in a big music hall, served en masse before enjoying the stage show with an old-time emcee. If you like Lawrence Welk, you're in for a treat. But for most travelers, these are painfully cheesy.

In the New Town (next to the National Portrait Gallery), the **Spirit of Scotland Show** runs a few nights each week in the summer (£75 for dinner and show, check details and book online, 5 Queen Street—see map on page 109, +44 131 618 9899, https:// spiritofscotlandshow.com).

The Princes Street Gardens Dancers perform a range of Scottish country dancing each summer at the Princes Street Gardens. The volunteer troupe demonstrates each dance, then invites spectators to give it a try (at Ross Bandstand in Princes Street Gardens—in the glen just below Edinburgh Castle—see map on page 109, +44 131 228 8616, www.princesstreetgardensdancing.org.uk). The same group offers summer programs in other parts of town (see website for details).

South of the center, **Taste of Scotland at Prestonfield House,** filling a kind of circus tent near the Dalkeith Road B&Bs, offers a kitschy folk evening with or without dinner Sunday to Friday. It's been closed but may reopen by the time you visit. Call or check online to see if reservations are being accepted and to confirm details. It's in the stables of "the handsomest house in Edinburgh," also home to the recommended Rhubarb Restaurant (Priestfield Road—see map on page 104, tel. +44 131 225 7800, www. scottishshow.co.uk)www.scottishshow.co.uk.

Theater

Even outside festival time, Edinburgh is a fine place for lively and affordable theater and live music. For a rundown of what's on, see www.list.co.uk.

▲▲Live Music in Pubs

While traditional music venues have been eclipsed by beer-focused student bars, Edinburgh still has a few good pubs that can deliver a traditional folk-music fix. Unless otherwise noted, the following

EDINBURGH

places are open daily and get going around 21:00 or 22:00 (sometimes a bit earlier); check their websites or drop by to ask for details. Many places that advertise "live music" offer only a solo singer/guitarist rather than a folk group. The monthly *Gig Guide* (free at TI, accommodations, and pubs, www.gigguide.co.uk) lists several places each night that have live music, divided by genre (pop, rock, world, and folk). For locations, see the "Edinburgh City Center Eateries" map, later.

Classic Music Pubs South of the Royal Mile:

For a musical pub crawl, do a loop of these three options—which are some of the most reliably good spots in town for traditional folk music.

Tight, stuffy **Sandy Bell's** offers frequent live folk music. There's no food, drinks are cheap, tables are small, and the vibe is local. They often have sessions both in the afternoon and in the evening—typically at 16:30 (Sat at 14:00, Mon at 17:30) and again at 21:30 (near the National Museum of Scotland at 25 Forrest Road, +44 131 225 2751, www.sandybellsedinburgh.co.uk).

Captain's Bar, with a pleasantly salty nautical theme, is a crowded-but-cozy, music-focused pub with live sessions of folk and traditional music nightly (closed Mon, 4 South College Street, https://captainsedinburgh.webs.com).

The Royal Oak, a characteristic, snug place for a dose of folk and blues, feels like a friend's living room (just off South Bridge opposite Chambers Road at 1 Infirmary Street, +44 131 557 2976, www.royal-oak-folk.com).

Grassmarket Neighborhood

This area below the castle bustles with live music and rowdy people spilling out of pubs and into what was (once upon a time) a busy market square. While it used to be a mecca for Scottish folk music, today it's more youthful with a heavy-drinking, rowdy feel...not really for serious folk connoisseurs. Still, it can be fun to wander through this lively area late at night and check out the scene. Thanks to the music and crowds, you'll know where to go...and where not to.

The Fiddlers Arms has a charming Grassmarket pub energy with live folk, pop, or rock, depending on the night (Thu-Sat from 21:00, at the far end of the square). Check out **Biddy Mulligans** or **White Hart Inn** (both on Grassmarket and both usually with a single Irish folk singer nightly). **Finnegans Wake,** on Victoria Street (which leads down to Grassmarket), is more of a down-and-dirty, classic rock bar with dancing. **The Bow Bar,** a couple doors away on Victoria Street, has no music but offers a hard-to-resist classic pub scene.

On the Royal Mile

The Scotsman's Lounge, just a few steps off the Royal Mile down Cockburn Street, may be the most central spot to find good folk music. Despite its touristy location, the clientele feels local. It's also a rare spot where you can often find afternoon sessions—starting at 17:00—rather than just later in the evening (73 Cockburn Street, +44 131 225 7726, www.thescotmanslounge.co.uk).

Nearby, three characteristic pubs within a few steps of each other on High Street (opposite the Radisson Blu Hotel) offer a fun setting, classic pub architecture and ambience, and live music (generally a single loud folk guitarist) for the cost of a beer: **Whiski Bar** (mostly trad and folk, www.whiskibar.co.uk), **Royal Mile** (classic pop, www.royalmiletavern.com), and **Mitre Bar** (acoustic pop/rock with some trad; usually weekends only).

Just a block away (on South Bridge) is **Whistle Binkies Live Music Bar.** While they rarely do folk or Scottish trad, this is the most serious of the music pubs, with an actual stage and several acts nightly (schedule posted inside the door makes the genre clear; young crowd, fun energy, sticky floors, no cover, +44 131 557 5114, www.whistlebinkies.com).

Farther down the Royal Mile, **No. 1 High Street** is an accessible little pub with a love of folk and traditional music (1 High Street, +44 131 556 5758). **World's End,** across the street, also has music many nights (4 High Street, +44 131 556 3628).

South of the Center, Near the B&B Neighborhood

The pubs in the B&B area don't typically have live music, but some are fun evening hangouts (for locations, see the "B&Bs & Restaurants South of the City Center" map, later).

Leslie's Bar, sitting between a working-class and an upper-class neighborhood, has two sides. Originally, the gang (men) would go in on the right to gather around the great hardwood bar, glittering with a century of *Cheers* ambience. Meanwhile, the more delicate folk (women) would slip in on the left, with its discreet doors, plush snugs (cozy private booths), and ornate ordering windows. Since 1896, this Victorian classic has been appreciated for both its real ales and its huge selection of fine whiskies (listed on a lengthy menu). Dive into the whisky mosh pit on the right, and let them show you how whisky can become "a very good friend" (daily 11:00-24:00, 49 Ratcliffe Terrace, +44 131 667 7205).

Other good pubs in this area include **The Old Bell** (uphill from Leslie's, popular and cozy, with big TV screens) and **The Salisbury Arms** (bigger, more sprawling, feels upscale); both are described later, under "Eating in Edinburgh."

Sleeping in Edinburgh

I've recommended accommodations in three areas: the city center, the West End, and a quieter neighborhood south of town.

To stay in the city center, you'll select from large hotels and mostly impersonal guesthouses. The West End (just a few blocks from the New Town, spanning from Haymarket to Charlotte Square) offers a few comfortable and more intimate hotels and guesthouses. These places provide a calm retreat in a central location.

For the classic B&B experience (friendly hosts and great cooked breakfasts), and something less expensive than a downtown hotel, look south of town near Dalkeith Road, Mayfield Gardens, or Mayfield Road. From this area, it's a long walk to the city center (about 30 minutes) or a quick bus or taxi/Uber ride.

Note that during the Festival in August, Edinburgh hotel and B&B prices skyrocket and most places do not accept bookings for one- or even two-night stays. If coming in August, book far in advance. Conventions, rugby matches, school holidays, and weekends can make finding a room tough at other times of year, too. In winter, when demand is light, some B&Bs close, and prices at all accommodations get soft.

HOTELS IN THE CITY CENTER

These places are mostly characterless, but they're close to the sight-seeing action and Edinburgh's excellent restaurant and pub scene. Prices are very high in peak season and drop substantially off-season (a good time to shop around). In each case, I'd skip the institutional breakfast and eat out. You'll generally pay about £10 a day to park near these hotels.

$$$$ The Inn on the Mile is your trendy, super-central option, filling a renovated old bank building right in the heart of the Royal Mile (at North Bridge/South Bridge). The nine bright and stylish rooms are an afterthought to the busy upmarket pub, which is where you'll check in. If you don't mind some noise (from the pub and the busy street) and climbing lots of stairs, it's a handy home base (breakfast extra, air-con, 82 High Street, +44 131 556 9940, www.theinnonthemile.co.uk, info@theinnonthemile.co.uk).

$$$$ Grassmarket Hotel's 42 rooms are quirky and fun, from the dandy comic-book wallpaper to the giant wall map of Edinburgh equipped with planning-your-visit magnets. The hotel is in a great location right on Grassmarket overlooking the Covenanters Memorial and above Biddy Mulligans Bar (family rooms, elevator serves half the rooms, 94 Grassmarket, +44 131 220 2299, www.grassmarkethotel.co.uk).

$$$ The Place Hotel has a fine New Town location 10 minutes north of the train station. This impersonal choice occupies three grand Georgian townhouses, with no elevator and long flights of stairs leading up to the 47 contemporary, no-frills rooms. Their outdoor terrace with retractable roof and heaters is a popular place to unwind (save money with a smaller city double, 34 York Place, +44 131 556 7575, www.placehotels.co.uk, frontdesk@yorkplace-edinburgh.co.uk). Their sister hotel, **$$$$ The Inn Place,** is super-centrally located in the heart of the Old Town, and may be reopening after a lengthy closure (check website for details).

$$$ Ten Hill Place Hotel is a 10-minute walk from the Royal Mile, down a quiet courtyard. It's owned by the 500-year-old Royal College of Surgeons, and profits go toward the college's important work and charitable goals. Its 129 rooms are classy, and some have views of the Salisbury Crags (breakfast extra, family rooms, elevator, 10 Hill Place, +44 131 662 2080, www.tenhillplace.com, reservations@tenhillplace.com).

$$ Motel One Edinburgh Royal, part of a stylish German budget-hotel chain, is between the train station and the Royal Mile; its 208 rooms feel upscale and trendy for its price range (pay more for a park view or less for a windowless "basic" room with skylight, breakfast extra, elevator, 18 Market Street, +44 131 220 0730, www.motel-one.com, edinburgh-royal@motel-one.com).

$$ Motel One Edinburgh Princes is a good deal for its location, with 140 rooms, some with nice views of Waverley Station and the Old Town. The rooms are cookie cutter, but the sprawling ballroom-like lounge offers great views (breakfast extra, family rooms, reception on first floor, elevator, 10 Princes Street, enter around the corner on West Register Street, +44 131 550 9220, www.motel-one.com, edinburgh-princes@motel-one.com).

Chain Hotels in the Center: Besides my recommendations above, you'll find a number of chain hotels close to the Royal Mile, including **Jurys Inn** (43 Jeffrey Street); **Adagio Aparthotel** (tempting location along the sleepier lower stretch of the Royal Mile at 231 Canongate); **Ibis Hotel** (three convenient branches: near the Tron Church, another around the corner along the busy South Bridge, and an Ibis Styles on St. Andrew Square in the New Town); **Holiday Inn Express** (two locations: just off the Royal Mile at 300 Cowgate and one on Picardy Place in the New Town), and **Travelodge Central** (just below the Royal Mile at 33 St. Mary's Street; additional locations in the New Town).

HOSTELS

¢ Baxter Hostel is an appealing boutique hostel. Occupying one floor of a Georgian townhouse (up several long, winding flights of stairs and below two more hostels), it has tons of ambience: tartan wallpaper, wood paneling, stone walls, decorative tile floors, and a

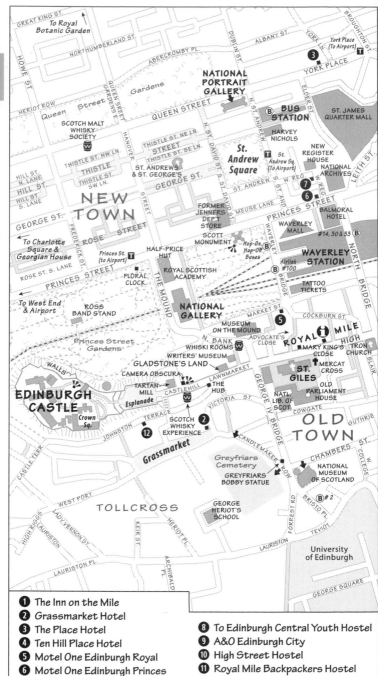

1 The Inn on the Mile
2 Grassmarket Hotel
3 The Place Hotel
4 Ten Hill Place Hotel
5 Motel One Edinburgh Royal
6 Motel One Edinburgh Princes
7 Baxter Hostel
8 To Edinburgh Central Youth Hostel
9 A&O Edinburgh City
10 High Street Hostel
11 Royal Mile Backpackers Hostel
12 Castle Rock Hostel

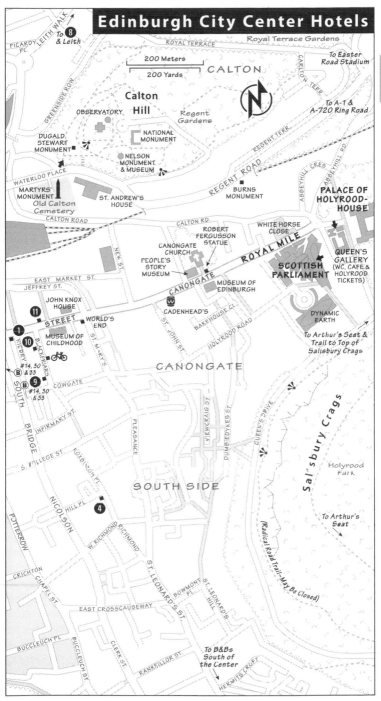

Edinburgh City Center Hotels

EDINBURGH

200 Meters
200 Yards

To & Leith

PICARDY PL.
LEITH WALK
GREENSIDE ROW
ROYAL TERRACE
Royal Terrace Gardens
To Easter Road Stadium
CALTON
CARLTON TERR.
Calton Hill
OBSERVATORY
Regent Gardens
DUGALD STEWART MONUMENT
NATIONAL MONUMENT
To A-1 & A-720 Ring Road
NELSON MONUMENT & MUSEUM
REGENT TERR.
ABBEYHILL RD.
ABBEYHILL CRES.
WATERLOO PLACE
MARTYRS' MONUMENT
ST. ANDREW'S HOUSE
Old Calton Cemetery
REGENT ROAD
BURNS MONUMENT
PALACE OF HOLYROOD-HOUSE
CALTON ROAD
CALTON RD.
NEW ST.
EAST MARKET ST.
JEFFREY ST.
WHITE HORSE CLOSE
ROBERT FERGUSSON STATUE
CANONGATE CHURCH
PEOPLE'S STORY MUSEUM
ROYAL MILE
SCOTTISH PARLIAMENT
QUEEN'S GALLERY (WC, CAFE & HOLYROOD TICKETS)
MUSEUM OF EDINBURGH
CANONGATE
CADENHEAD'S
DYNAMIC EARTH
JOHN KNOX HOUSE
WORLD'S END
ST. MARY'S ST.
BAKEHOUSE CL.
ST. JOHN ST.
HOLYROOD ROAD
To Arthur's Seat & Trail to Top of Salisbury Crags
MUSEUM OF CHILDHOOD
BLACKFRIARS ST.
NIDDRY ST.
#14, 30 & 33
COWGATE
#14, 30 & 33
S. COLLEGE ST.
INFIRMARY ST.
CANONGATE
PLEASANCE
VIEWCRAIG ST.
DUMBIEDYKES ST.
QUEEN'S DRIVE
Salisbury Crags
Holyrood Park
SOUTH BRIDGE
NICOLSON
HILL PL.
ROXBURGH PL.
W. RICHMOND ST.
RICHMOND ST.
SOUTH SIDE
ST. LEONARD'S HILL
ST. LEONARD'S ST.
(Radical Road Trail—May Be Closed)
To Arthur's Seat
POTTERROW
CRICHTON ST.
CHAPEL ST.
EAST CROSSCAUSEWAY
BOWMONT PL.
BUCCLEUCH PL.
BUCCLEUCH ST.
CLERK ST.
RANKEILLOR ST.
HERMITS CROFT
To B&Bs South of the Center

beautifully restored kitchen/lounge that you'd want in your own house. Space is tight—hallways are snug, and five dorms (42 beds) share one bathroom. Another room, with four beds, has its own en-suite bathroom (includes scrambled-egg breakfast; small fee for towel, travel adapters, and locks; 5 West Register Street, +44 131 503 1001, www.thebaxterhostel.com, thehost@thebaxterhostel. com).

¢ **Edinburgh Central Youth Hostel** rents 251 beds in 72 rooms accommodating three to six people (all with private bathrooms and lockers). Guests can eat cheaply in the cafeteria, or cook for the cost of groceries in the members' kitchen (private rooms available, pay laundry, 15-minute downhill walk from Waverley Station—head down Leith Walk, pass through two roundabouts, hostel is on your left—or take bus #22 to Annadale Street or #25 to Leopold Place, 9 Haddington Place off Leith Walk, +44 131 524 2090, www.hostellingscotland.org.uk, central@hostellingscotland. org.uk).

¢ **A&O Edinburgh City,** part of a German chain, is just off the Royal Mile and rents 272 bunks. Dorm rooms have 4 to 12 beds, and there are also a few private singles and twin rooms (all rooms have private bathrooms). Bar 50 in the basement has an inviting lounge. Half of the rooms function as a university dorm during the school year, becoming available just in time for the tourists (breakfast extra, kitchen, laundry, free daily walking tour, 50 Blackfriars Street, +44 131 524 1989, www.aohostels.com).

¢ **Cheap and Scruffy Bohemian Hostels in the Center:** These three sister hostels—popular crash pads for young, hip backpackers—are beautifully located in the noisy center (some locations also have private rooms, www.macbackpackers.com): **High Street Hostel** (150 beds, 8 Blackfriars Street, just off High Street/Royal Mile, +44 131 557 3984); **Royal Mile Backpackers** (38 beds, 105 High Street, +44 131 557 6120); and **Castle Rock Hostel** (300 beds, just below the castle and above the pubs, 15 Johnston Terrace, +44 131 225 9666).

THE WEST END

The area just west of the New Town and Charlotte Square is a quiet, classy, residential area of stately Georgian buildings. Hotels here can be pricey and ostentatious, catering mostly to business travelers. But my recommendations are central and offer character and hospitality. Though these places aren't as intimate as my recommended B&Bs south of town, the West End is convenient to most sightseeing. It's an easy 10- to 15-minute walk to bustling Princes Street. (For a quicker approach to the Royal Mile—without the steep hike—you can curl around the back of the castle on

EDINBURGH

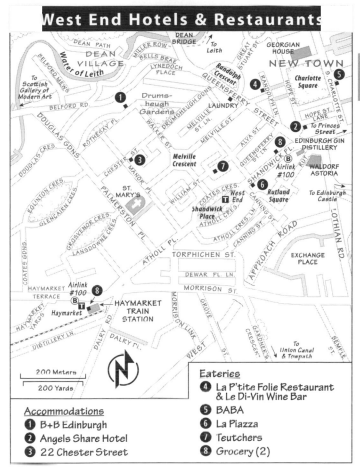

West End Hotels & Restaurants

DEAN PATH
DEAN BRIDGE
To Leith
GEORGIAN HOUSE
NEW TOWN
DEAN VILLAGE
Water of Leith
MILLER ROW
BELLS BRAE
LYNEDOCH PLACE
Randolph Crescent
QUEENSFERRY
GREAT STUART ST.
RANDOLPH ST.
Charlotte Square
HOPE ST.
CHARLOTTE ST.

⑤

To Scottish Gallery of Modern Art
①
Drums-heugh Gardens
BELFORD RD.
LAUNDRY
MELVILLE ST. LN.
MELVILLE ST.
ALVA ST.
HOPE ST. LANE
② To Princes Street →
QUEENSFERRY ST. LN.
④

DOUGLAS GDNS
ROTHESAY PL.
CHESTER ST.
MANOR PL.
WALKER ST.
DRUMSHEUGH GDNS.
⑧
EDINBURGH GIN DISTILLERY

DOUGLAS CRES.
③
Melville Crescent
Airlink #100
WALDORF ASTORIA

EGLINTON CRES.
ST. MARY'S
WILLIAM ST.
⑦
COATES CRES.
SHANDWICK PL.
RUTLAND ST.
⑥
Rutland Square
To Edinburgh Castle

PALMERSTON PL.
West End
CANNING ST.

GLENCAIRN CRES.
Shandwick Place
ATHOLL CRES.

GROSVENOR CRES.
LANSDOWNE CRES.
ATHOLL PL.
ATHOLL CRES. LN.
CANNING ST.
APPROACH ROAD
LOTHIAN RD.

COATES GDNS.
TORPHICHEN ST.
EXCHANGE PLACE

DEWAR PL. LN.

HAYMARKET TERRACE
Airlink #100
⑧
MORRISON ST.
GROVE ST.
SEMPLE ST.

HAYMARKET YARDS
Haymarket
HAYMARKET TRAIN STATION
DALRY RD.
DALRY PL.
MORRISON LINK
WEST
GARDNER'S CRESCENT
To Union Canal & Towpath

DISTILLERY LN.

N

200 Meters

200 Yards

Accommodations
① B+B Edinburgh
② Angels Share Hotel
③ 22 Chester Street

Eateries
④ La P'tite Folie Restaurant & Le Di-Vin Wine Bar
⑤ BABA
⑥ La Piazza
⑦ Teutchers
⑧ Grocery (2)

King's Stables Road to reach Grassmarket in about 10 minutes, then huff up scenic Victoria Street.)

To get here from the train station, take the Airlink #100 from Waverley Bridge to Shandwick Place, or take the train to Haymarket Station (depending on your hotel—confirm in advance). Coming from Princes Street or the airport, take the tram to the West End stop.

$$$$ B+B Edinburgh is a classic, upscale boutique hotel with 27 comfortable rooms; the ones in back have grand views over Dean Village and the outskirts of Edinburgh. The public spaces (including a museum-like library) are stately and impressive, and it's situated on quiet Rothesay Terrace, where you'll feel like a diplomat retreating to your private suite (family rooms, elevator,

3 Rothesay Terrace, +44 131 225 5084, www.bb-edinburgh.com, info@bb-edinburgh.com).

$$$$ Angels Share Hotel is a cheerful, well-run, inviting place with a proud Scottish heritage. Each of its tidy, stylish 31 rooms is named after a contemporary Scottish figure (his or her portrait hangs above your bed). The attached bar serves a great breakfast and has live music on weekends (elevator, 11 Hope Street, +44 131 247 7007, www.angelssharehotel.com, reception@angelssharehotel.com).

$$ 22 Chester Street offers a mix of Georgian charm and Ikea comfort, renting five smartly appointed rooms near St. Mary's Cathedral. The lounge is an elegant and cozy place to unwind. Two rooms have private bathrooms down the hall, and a couple rooms are below street level but get plenty of light (RS%, family rooms, no breakfast but lounge has stocked fridge and microwave, street parking only, 22 Chester Street, +44 7872 944 710, https://22chesterstreetedinburgh.co.uk, marypremiercru@gmail.com, owner Mary and manager Lukasz).

B&Bs SOUTH OF THE CITY CENTER

A B&B generally provides more warmth and lower prices. At these not-quite-interchangeable places, character is provided by the personality quirks of the hosts and sometimes the decor. In general, cash is preferred and can lead to discounted rates. Book direct—you will pay a much higher rate through a booking website.

Near the B&Bs, you'll find plenty of fine eateries and some good, classic pubs. A few places have their own private parking; others offer access to easy, free street parking (ask when booking—or better yet, don't rent a car for your time in Edinburgh). The nearest launderette is Ace Cleaning Centre (see "Helpful Hints" at the beginning of this chapter).

Taxi or Uber fare between the city center and these B&Bs is about £8-10. If taking the bus from the B&Bs into the city, hop off at the South Bridge stop for the Royal Mile.

Near Dalkeith Road

Most of my B&Bs near Dalkeith Road are located south of the Royal Commonwealth Pool. This comfortable, safe neighborhood is a 10-minute bus ride from the Royal Mile.

To get here from the train station, catch the bus around the corner on North Bridge: Use the escalators to exit the station onto Princes Street, turn right, continue around the corner onto North Bridge, cross the street, and walk up the bridge to the bus stop (lines #14, #30, or #33). Confirm your bus stop with your B&B.

$$$ Hotel Ceilidh-Donia is bigger (17 rooms) and more hotel-like than other nearby B&Bs, with a bar and a small reception area, but managers Kevin and Susan and their staff provide guesthouse warmth. The back deck is a pleasant place to relax on a warm day. The name—a pun on *"ceilidh"* and "Caledonia"—is pronounced "kayley-donya" (family room, 2-night minimum on peak-season weekends, 14 Marchhall Crescent, +44 131 667 2743, www.hotelceilidh-donia.co.uk, reservations@hotelceilidh-donia.co.uk).

$$ Gifford House, on busy Dalkeith Road, is a bright, flowery retreat with six peaceful, colorful rooms (some with ornate cornices and views of Arthur's Seat) and compact, modern bathrooms (RS% with cash, family rooms, street parking, 103 Dalkeith Road, +44 131 667 4688, www.edinburghbedbreakfast.co.uk, giffordhouse@btinternet.com; Margaret, David, and Melanie).

$$ Ard-Na-Said B&B, in an elegant 1875 Victorian house, has seven bright, spacious rooms with modern bathrooms, including one ground-floor room with a pleasant patio and two with Ard-Na-Said (Arthur's Seat) views (2-night minimum preferred in summer, off-street parking, 5 Priestfield Road, +44 131 283 6524, mobile +44 747 660 6202, www.ardnasaid.co.uk, info@ardnasaid.co.uk, Audrey Ballantine and her son Steven).

$$ AmarAgua Guest House is an inviting Victorian home away from home, with six welcoming rooms—a couple with four-poster beds—and eager hosts (one double has private bath down the hall, 2-night minimum, no kids under 12, street parking, 10 Kilmaurs Terrace, +44 131 667 6775, www.amaragua.co.uk, reservations@amaragua.co.uk, Lucia and Kuan).

$ Airdenair Guest House is a hands-off, bare-bones guest-house, with no formal host greeting (you'll get an access code to let yourself in) and a self-serve breakfast buffet. But the price is right, and the seven simple rooms—some with older bathrooms—do the trick (29 Kilmaurs Road, +44 781 731 3035, www.airdenair.co.uk, contact@airdenair.co.uk, Duncan).

On or near Mayfield Gardens

These higher-end places are just a couple of blocks from the Dalkeith Road options, along the busy Newington Road (which turns into Mayfield Gardens). All have private parking. To reach them from the center, hop on bus #3, #7, #8, #29, #31, #37, or #49. Note: Some buses depart from the second bus stop, a bit farther along North Bridge.

$$$ At 23 Mayfield Guest House, Ross and Kathleen (with their wee helpers Ethan and Alfie) rent seven splurge-worthy,

EDINBURGH

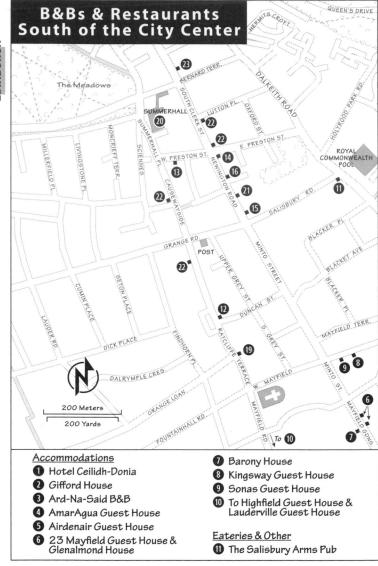

B&Bs & Restaurants South of the City Center

Accommodations

1. Hotel Ceilidh-Donia
2. Gifford House
3. Ard-Na-Said B&B
4. AmarAgua Guest House
5. Airdenair Guest House
6. 23 Mayfield Guest House & Glenalmond House
7. Barony House
8. Kingsway Guest House
9. Sonas Guest House
10. To Highfield Guest House & Lauderville Guest House

Eateries & Other

11. The Salisbury Arms Pub

thoughtfully appointed rooms complete with high-tech bathrooms (rain showers and motion-sensor light-up mirrors). Little extras—such as locally sourced gourmet breakfasts, an inviting guest lounge outfitted with leather-bound Sir Arthur Conan Doyle books, an "honesty bar," and classic black-and-white movie screenings—make you feel like royalty (RS% with cash, family room, 2-night minimum preferred in summer, 23 Mayfield Gardens, +44 131 667 5806, www.23mayfield.co.uk, info@23mayfield.co.uk).

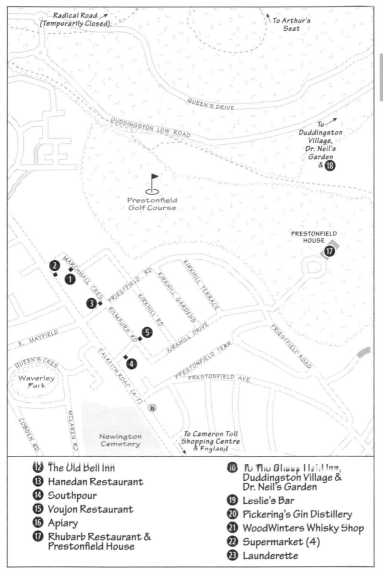

$$$ **Barony House** is run with infectious enthusiasm by Aussies Paul and Susan. Susan has decorated the place with incredible care, with many handmade flourishes that revive the house's historical character while injecting it with fun and style—and she also cooks a wonderful variety of breakfasts. Paul enjoys chatting with guests and telling the story of how their family wound up in Edinburgh. They have six elegant doubles, including two in the "garden" level next door, in a former servants' quarters—now a peaceful re-

treat with access to a shared kitchen (3-night minimum preferred in summer, no kids under 9, 20 Mayfield Gardens, +44 131 662 9938, www.baronyhouse.co.uk, booknow@baronyhouse.co.uk).

$$$ Glenalmond House, run by Jimmy and Fiona Mackie, has nine smart rooms, two with garden patios (RS% with cash, discounts for longer stays, family room, no kids under 5, 25 Mayfield Gardens, +44 131 668 2392, www.glenalmondhouse.com, enquiries@glenalmondhouse.com).

$$ Kingsway Guest House, with seven bright and stylish rooms, is owned by conscientious, delightful Gary and Lizzie, who have thought of all the little touches, such as in-room internet radios, and offer good advice on neighborhood eats (RS% with cash, family rooms, one room with private bath down the hall, off-street parking, 5 East Mayfield, +44 131 667 5029, https://edinburgh-guesthouse.com, booking@kingswayguesthouse.com).

$$ Sonas Guest House is nothing fancy—just a simple, easygoing place with nine rooms, six of which have bathtubs (no cooked breakfast, family room, 3 East Mayfield, +44 131 664 3170, www.sonasguesthouse.com, info@sonasguesthouse.com, Irene and Dennis).

On Mayfield Road

These accommodations are just one block over from Mayfield Gardens (described above). While you can catch bus #42 from here into the center, it's usually easier just to walk a few minutes over to Mayfield Gardens and hop on one of the buses listed above.

$$$ Highfield Guest House feels a bit more refined, with five rooms, crisp decor, and white tablecloths in the breakfast room (one single has a private shower on the hall, street parking, 83 Mayfield Road, +44 131 667 8717, www.highfieldgh.co.uk, info@highfieldgh.co.uk; Maggie, Gordon, and Kate).

$$ Lauderville Guest House, run by upbeat Simon, has seven rooms with modern flourishes (2- or 3-night minimum in peak times, family room, private parking, 52 Mayfield Road, +44 7887 648 111, www.laudervilleguesthouse.co.uk, reservation@laudervilleguesthouse.co.uk).

Eating in Edinburgh

Edinburgh is thriving with dining options. Tourists clog the famous stretches where bottom-feeding eateries make easy money. But if you walk just a few blocks away from the chain restaurants and tacky strips, you'll find a different world. Things are very competitive, and you'll find even high-end places offer specials for lunch and sometimes early dinner. Reservations are essential in August and on weekends, and a good idea anytime. Here are some favorites of mine, designed to fill the tank economically at lunch time or give you a great experience for dinner. With the ease and economy of Uber and the bus system, don't be too tied to your hotel or B&B neighborhood for dinner.

THE OLD TOWN

I prefer spots within a few minutes' walk of the tourist zone—just far enough to offer better value and a more local atmosphere.

Just off the Royal Mile on George IV Bridge

$$$ Le Bistrot is the tour guides' favorite—a delightful café hiding just steps off of the Royal Mile in the same building as the French consulate (as if put here by the consulate to promote a love of French culture). Its glowy ambience, authentic French menu, and great prices make this a welcoming spot to have dinner before an evening stroll down the Royal Mile—when all the crowds have gone to the pubs. Try their soup or fish of the day (affordable fixed-price lunch, daily 9:00-22:00, 59 George IV Bridge, +44 131 225 4021).

$$$$ Ondine Seafood Restaurant is a dressy, top-end restaurant with a smart clientele and a quality, sophisticated vibe; it's known for some of the best seafood in town (the menu is almost exclusively seafood). It's a block off the Royal Mile, upstairs in a modern building with a sleek dining room that overlooks the busy road, but feels a world apart. If you're looking for deals, oysters are £2.50 each at the bar during happy hour (Tue-Sat 12:00-15:00 & 17:30-22:00, closed Sun-Mon, 2 George IV Bridge, +44 131 226 1888, www.ondinerestaurant.co.uk).

$$$ The Outsider has a thriving energy. It's a proudly independent bistro with a social (noisy) vibe filling its sleek, sprawling dining room. The menu features good-value, fresh, modern Scottish cuisine with daily specials "until sold out" scribbled on it. You feel like a winner eating here. Ask for a window table at the back for views of the castle floating above the rooftops (daily 12:00-23:00, long list of lunches under £10 available until 17:00, reservations smart, 15 George IV Bridge, +44 131 226 3131, www.theoutsiderrestaurant.com, Eddie and partners).

Along the Royal Mile, Downhill from St. Giles' Cathedral

Though the eateries along this most-crowded stretch of the city are invariably touristy, the scene is fun. Sprinkled in this list are some places a block or two off the main drag offering better values and maybe fewer tourists.

$$$ Devil's Advocate is a popular gastropub that hides down the narrow lane called Advocates Close, directly across the Royal

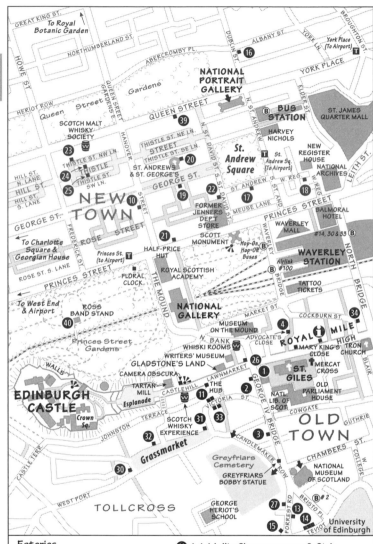

Eateries

1. Le Bistrot
2. Ondine Seafood Restaurant
3. The Outsider
4. Devil's Advocate
5. Wedgwood Restaurant
6. David Bann Vegetarian Rest.
7. Edinburgh Larder
8. Mimi's Little Bakehouse
9. Clarinda's Tea Room
10. Oink (2)
11. I.J. Mellis Cheesemonger & Oink
12. The Haggis Box
13. Union of Genius & Mums
14. Ting Thai Caravan, Saboteur & El Cartel
15. Civerinos Slice
16. The Magnum Restaurant & Bar
17. Dishoom
18. Café Royal
19. The Dome Restaurant
20. St. Andrew's & St. George's Church Undercroft Café

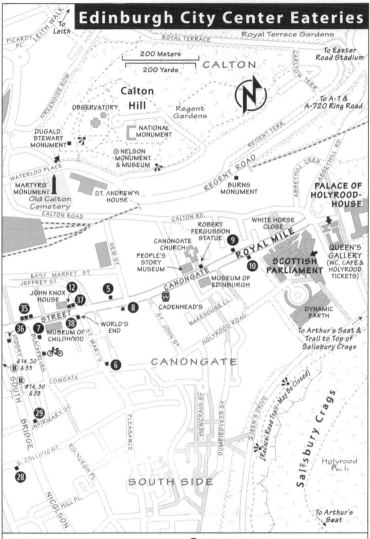

Edinburgh City Center Eateries

200 Meters
200 Yards

To Leith

To Easter Road Stadium

To A-1 & A-720 Ring Road

CALTON

Calton Hill

ROYAL TERRACE
Royal Terrace Gardens

PICARDY PL.

LEITH WALK

GREENSIDE ROW

OBSERVATORY

Regent Gardens

NATIONAL MONUMENT

DUGALD STEWART MONUMENT

NELSON MONUMENT & MUSEUM

CARLTON TERR.

REGENT TERR.

WATERLOO PLACE

MARTYRS' MONUMENT

Old Calton Cemetery

ST. ANDREW'S HOUSE

CALTON ROAD

REGENT ROAD

BURNS MONUMENT

ABBEYHILL CRES.

ABBEYHILL RD.

PALACE OF HOLYROOD-HOUSE

EAST MARKET ST.

JEFFREY ST.

NEW ST.

CALTON RD.

WHITE HORSE CLOSE

ROBERT FERGUSSON STATUE

CANONGATE CHURCH

PEOPLE'S STORY MUSEUM

CANONGATE

MUSEUM OF EDINBURGH

ROYAL MILE

⑨

⑩

SCOTTISH PARLIAMENT

QUEEN'S GALLERY (WC, CAFE & HOLYROOD TICKETS)

JOHN KNOX HOUSE

⑫

③⑦

⑤

⑧

CADENHEAD'S

BAKEHOUSE CL.

ST. JOHN ST.

HOLYROOD ROAD

DYNAMIC EARTH

To Arthur's Seat & Trail to Top of Salisbury Crags

�35

㊱

⑦

MUSEUM OF CHILDHOOD

STREET

BLACKFRIARS

③⑧

WORLD'S END

ST. MARY'S

⑥

CANONGATE

#14, 30 & 33

#14, 30 & 33

SOUTH BRIDGE

KIDD'Y ST.

COWGATE

INFIRMARY ST.

PLEASANCE

VIEWCRAIG ST.

DUMBIEDYKES RD.

QUEEN'S DRIVE

Radical Road Trail—May Be Closed

Salisbury Crags

Holyrood Park

㉙

S. COLLEGE ST.

DRUMMOND ST.

㉘

NICOLSON ST.

ROXBURGH PL.

NICOLSON HILL PL.

SOUTH SIDE

To Arthur's Seat

㉑ Marks & Spencer Food Hall
㉒ Sainsbury's
㉓ Le Café St. Honoré
㉔ The Bon Vivant
㉕ Fishers in the City

<u>Pubs & Nightlife</u>
㉖ Deacon Brodie's Tavern
㉗ Sandy Bell's Pub
㉘ Captain's Bar
㉙ The Royal Oak Pub

㉚ The Fiddlers Arms
㉛ Biddy Mulligans
㉜ White Hart Inn
㉝ Finnegans Wake & The Bow Bar
㉞ The Scotsman's Lounge
㉟ Whiski Bar, Royal Mile, Mitre Bar
㊱ Whistle Binkies Bar
㊲ No. 1 High Street Pub
㊳ The World's End Pub
㊴ Spirit of Scotland Show
㊵ Princes Street Gardens Dancers

Mile from St. Giles. With an old cellar setting—exposed stone and heavy beams—done up in modern style, it feels like a mix of old and new Edinburgh. Creative whisky cocktails kick off a menu that dares to be adventurous, but with a respect for Scottish tradition (daily 12:00-22:00, 9 Advocates Close, +44 131 225 4465).

$$$$ Wedgwood Restaurant is romantic, contemporary, chic, and as gourmet as possible with no pretense. Paul Wedgwood cooks while his wife Lisa serves with appetizing charm. The cuisine: creative, modern Scottish with an international twist. They're known for their scallop and roe deer, or consider their "Wee Tour of Scotland" tasting *menu* for £65. Paul and Lisa believe in making the meal the event of the evening—don't come here to eat and run (the table is yours). I like the ground level with the Royal Mile view and the busy kitchen ambience better than their basement seating (lunch specials, fine wine by the glass; Wed-Sun 12:00-15:00 & 18:00-22:00, closed Mon-Tue; reservations smart, 267 Canongate on Royal Mile, +44 131 558 8737, www.wedgwoodtherestaurant. co.uk).

$$ David Bann Vegetarian Restaurant is a worthwhile stop for well-heeled vegetarians in need of a break from traditional veggie grub. While vegetarian as can be, this place—with its candles and woody decor—doesn't have even a hint of hippie. It's upscale (it has a cocktail bar), sleek, minimalist, and stylish (gorgeously presented dishes), serious about quality, and organic. There's an enthusiastic local following—and decadent desserts (daily 12:00-22:00, vegan and gluten-free options, a long block off the Royal Mile at 56 St. Mary's Street, +44 131 556 5888).

Quick, Easy, and Cheap Breakfast and Lunch Options

$$ Edinburgh Larder promises "a taste of the country" in the center of the city. With a hipster/granola aesthetic, they focus on high-quality, homestyle breakfast and lunches made from seasonal, local ingredients. The café, with table service, is a convivial space with rustic tables filled by local families. Their "Little Larder" sister outlet, next door, offers a shorter but similar menu (Mon-Fri 8:00-16:00, Sat-Sun from 9:00, 15 Blackfriars Street, +44 131 556 6922).

$ Mimi's Little Bakehouse, a handy Royal Mile outpost of a prizewinning bakery, serves up baked goods—try the scones—as well as soups, wraps, and sandwiches in their cute and modern shop (daily 9:00-17:00, 250 Canongate, +44 131 556 6632).

$ Clarinda's Tea Room, near the bottom of the Royal Mile, is a charming time warp—a fine and tasty place to relax after touring the Mile or the Palace of Holyroodhouse. Stop in for a quiche, salad, or soup lunch. It's also great for sandwiches and tea and cake any time (Tue-Sat 9:00-16:00, closed Sun-Mon, 69 Canongate, +44 131 557 1888).

$ Oink is handy for a cheap sandwich to go near the top (34 Victoria Street) or bottom (82 Canongate) of the Royal Mile. They carve from a freshly roasted pig each afternoon for sandwiches that come in "piglet," "oink," or "grunter" sizes (that's small, medium, large). Watch the pig shrink in the front window throughout the day (daily 11:00-17:00 or whenever they run out of meat, cash only, +44 777 196 8233). There's also a location in the New Town, at 38 Hanover Street (see later).

$ I.J. Mellis Cheesemonger, tucked down Victoria Street just off the top of the Royal Mile, stocks a wide variety of Scottish, English, and international cheeses. They're as knowledgeable about cheese as they are generous with samples. This is a great spot to pick up some high-quality cheese for a snack or picnic (daily 11:00-sometime between 17:30 and 19:00 depending on the day, 30A Victoria Street, +44 131 226 6215).

$ The Haggis Box—a food counter inside the lobby of the Scottish Storytelling Center—is the place for adventurous eaters who want to sample haggis. You can get haggis plus neeps and tatties (turnips and potatoes)—including a vegan version—for under £10, with interesting sauces; they also have soup of the day and quiche (daily 10:00-17:00, 43 High Street, +44 780 221 6987).

Historic Pubs for Grub Along the Mile

To grab some forgettable pub grub in historic surroundings, consider one of these landmark pubs described on my self-guided walk. All offer basic pub meals for around £10-15 (cheaper lunch deals) and serve food daily from about 12:00 to 21:00. Deacon Brodie's is the most touristy and famous. The others have better ambience and feature music at night (see "Live Music in Pubs" on page 93).

$$ Deacon Brodie's Tavern, at a dead-center location on the Royal Mile, has a sloppy pub on the ground floor with a sloppy restaurant upstairs (435 Lawnmarket).

$$ The Mitre Bar has a classic interior, and their menu includes good meat pies (131 High Street). The neighboring **$$ Whiski Bar** and **$$ Royal Mile Pub** are also good options.

$$ The World's End Pub, farther down the Mile at Canongate, is a colorful old place dishing up hearty meals from a creative menu in a fun, dark, and noisy space (4 High Street).

Near the National Museum

These restaurants (all within about 100 yards of each other) are happily removed from the Royal Mile melee and skew to a youthful clientele with few tourists. After passing the Greyfriars Bobby statue and the National Museum, fork right onto Forrest Road.

$ **Union of Genius** is a creative soup kitchen with a strong identity. They cook up a selection of delicious soups with fun foodie twists each morning at their main location in Leith, then deliver them to this shop by bicycle (for environmental reasons). These are supplemented with good salads and fresh-baked breads. The "flight" comes with three small cups of soup and three types of bread. Line up at the counter, then either take your soup to go or sit in the cramped interior, with a couple of tables and counter seating (Mon-Fri 11:00-16:00, closed Sat-Sun, 8 Forrest Road, +44 131 226 4436).

$$ **Mums,** a kitschy Scottish diner, serves up comfort food just like mum used to make. The extensive menu offers huge portions of heavy, greasy Scottish/British standards—bangers (sausages), meat pies, burgers, and artery-clogging breakfasts (served until 12:00)—and vegetarian options. There's often a line out the door on weekends (Mon-Sat 9:00-22:00, Sun from 10:00, 4 Forrest Road, +44 131 260 9806).

$$ **Ting Thai Caravan** is a loud, industrial-mod eatery serving adventurous Thai street food (soups, noodles, and curries). It's a young, stark, and simple place with thumping music, communal tables, and great food (daily 11:30-22:00, Fri-Sat until 23:00, 8 Teviot Place, +44 131 225 9801). There are other locations around Edinburgh, too.

$$ **Saboteur,** with the same owners and just a few doors down from Ting Thai Caravan, serves Vietnamese and Southeast Asian cuisine in a slightly more casual (but equally hip), techy-chic space. The enticing menu of bao buns and creative bowls encourages a sense of adventure—consider ordering family-style (no reservations, daily 11:30-22:00, Fri-Sat until 23:00, 19 Teviot Place, +44 131 623 0384).

Other places worth considering here include a branch of the local taqueria chain $$ **El Cartel,** and $ **Civerinos Slice,** selling pizza by the slice.

THE NEW TOWN

In the Georgian part of town, you'll find a bustling world of office workers, students, and pensioners doing their thing. These eateries are all within a 10-minute walk of Waverley Station.

Favorites on or near St. Andrew Square

In addition to the options listed below, St. Andrew Square is home to several Edinburgh branches of trendy London restaurants, including Gordon Ramsay's Bread Street Kitchen, Wagamama (Asian noodles), and Wahaca (Mexican).

$$$ **The Magnum Restaurant and Bar** is a relaxed, classy pub-gone-bistro serving beautifully presented Scottish dishes with

smart service and no pretense. The appetizing menu is creative and inviting. A block beyond the tourist zone, it feels like a neighborhood favorite (lunch specials, daily 12:00-14:30 & 17:30-22:00, 1 Albany Street, +44 131 557 4366).

$$$ Dishoom is a sprawling, high-energy, Bombay Café phenom. The menu makes Indian food joyfully accessible (and affordable). You'll enjoy upscale South Asian cuisine in a bustling, dark, 1920s dining room on the second floor overlooking St. Andrew Square; there are also a few outdoor tables (I'd avoid the basement). It's a popular spot but no reservations are taken after 17:45, so arrive early or plan to wait in a long line (daily 8:00-23:00, 3A St. Andrew Square, +44 131 202 6406).

$$ Café Royal is the perfect *fin de siècle* setting for a coffee, beer, or light meal. Drop in, if only to admire the 1880 tiles featuring famous inventors. The menu is both traditional and modern, with vegetarian dishes and lots of oysters (daily 12:00-22:00, 19 West Register Street, +44 131 556 1884, no reservations). The attached small, dressier **$$$$ restaurant,** specializing in oysters, fish, and game—while stuffier and more expensive—is also good.

$$$$ The Dome Restaurant, filling what was a fancy bank, serves modern international cuisine around a classy bar and under

the elegant 19th-century skylight dome. With soft jazz and chic, white-tablecloth ambience, it feels a world apart. Come here not for the food, but for the opulent atmosphere (lunch deals, early-bird special until 18:30, daily 12:00-23:00, reserve for dinner, open for a drink any time under the dome, 14 George Street, +44 131 624 8624, www.thedomeedinburgh.com).

$ St. Andrew's and St. George's Church Undercroft Café, in the basement of a fine old church, is the cheapest place in town for soup, sandwiches, quiche, or scones for lunch. Your tiny bill helps support the Church of Scotland (Mon-Fri 10:00-14:00, closed Sat-Sun, just off St. Andrew Square at 13 George Street, +44 131 225 3847). It's run by sweet volunteers who love to chat.

$ Oink—the pig roastery described earlier along the Royal Mile—also has a location in the heart of the New Town (daily 11:00-17:00 or until sold out, 38 Hanover Street).

Supermarkets: Marks & Spencer Food Hall offers an assortment of tasty hot foods, prepared sandwiches, fresh bakery items, a wide selection of wines and beverages, and plastic utensils at the checkout queue. It's just a block from the Scott Monument and the

EDINBURGH

picnic-perfect Princes Street Gardens (Mon-Sat 8:00-19:00, Thu until 20:00, Sun 11:00-18:00, Princes Street 54—separate stairway next to main M&S entrance leads directly to food hall, +44 131 225 2301). **Sainsbury's** supermarket, a block off Princes Street, offers grab-and-go items (daily 7:00-22:00, on corner of Rose Street on St. Andrew Square).

Hip Eateries on and near Thistle Street

Peaceful little Thistle Street has a cluster of enticing eateries. Browse the options, but tune into these favorites.

$$$ Le Café St. Honoré, tucked away like a secret bit of old Paris, is a charming place with friendly service and walls lined with wine bottles. It serves French-Scottish cuisine in tight, Old World, cut-glass elegance to a dressy crowd (two- and three-course lunch and dinner specials, Thu-Mon 12:00-14:00 & 17:30-21:00, closed Tue-Wed, reservations smart—I'd ask to sit upstairs rather than in the basement, 34 Northwest Thistle Street Lane, +44 131 226 2211, www.cafesthonore.com).

$$$ The Bon Vivant is woody, youthful, and candlelit, with a rotating menu of French/Scottish dishes, lots of champagne by the glass, and a companion wine shop next door. They have fun tapas plates and heartier dishes, served either in the bar up front or in the restaurant in back (daily 12:00-22:00, 55 Thistle Street, +44 131 225 3275).

$$$ Fishers in the City, a good place to dine on seafood, has an inviting menu and lots of nice wines by the glass. The energy is lively, the clientele is smart, and the room is bright and airy with a simple elegance (daily 12:00-22:00, reservations smart, 58 Thistle Street, +44 131 225 5109, www.fishersrestaurants.co.uk).

THE WEST END

In this posh neighborhood of high-end eateries, the following places have character, tasty food, and fair prices. For locations, see the map on page 101.

$$$ La P'tite Folie Restaurant occupies a quirky, half-timbered Tudor house that once housed a Polish Catholic church. Its sophisticated, local clientele goes for flavorful specialties like steak and duck—all with a French flair (good-value two-course lunch; food served Tue-Thu 12:00-15:00 & 18:00-22:00, Fri-Sat until 23:00, closed Sun-Mon; reservations smart, 9 Randolph Place, +44 131 225 8678, www.laptitefolie.co.uk). Under the same roof, **$$ Le Di-Vin Wine Bar** is in the nave of the church, with an extensive wine list and nice cheese-and-meat boards (Mon-Sat 12:00-late, closed Sun, +44 131 538 1815).

$$$ BABA—technically in the New Town (facing Charlotte Square) but close to the West End—is a wonderful spot for charcoal-grilled, Lebanese-style small plates in a hip and trendy, ramshackle-chic atmosphere. As it's as popular as it is delicious, it's smart to book ahead (daily 12:00-21:30, in the Kimpton Hotel at 130 George Street, +44 131 527 4999, www.baba.restaurant).

$$ La Piazza stands out among several Italian restaurants in this neighborhood. It's a welcoming place with solid pasta dishes, pizzas, and an Italian villa vibe. Pleasant terrace tables are out back (Mon-Sat 12:00-14:30 & 17:00-22:00, closed Sun, 97 Shandwick Place, +44 131 221 1150).

$$ Teutchers is a friendly joint on cute William Street, with a fun vibe and nice tables in a rustic space. The food is a cut above typical pub grub (daily 12:00-21:30, 26 William Street, +44 131 225 2973).

Supermarket: There's a handy **Sainsbury's** near my recommended West End accommodations (daily 6:00-23:00, 32 Shandwick Place). A **Marks & Spencer** is at the Haymarket train station (Mon-Fri 7:00-21:00, Thu-Fri until 22:00, Sun 9:00-20:00).

IN THE B&B NEIGHBORHOOD, TO THE SOUTH

These places are within a 10-minute walk of my recommended B&Bs. For locations, see the map on page 104. For a cozy drink after dinner, visit the recommended pubs in the area (see "Nightlife in Edinburgh," earlier). Except for the "memorable meals" places, I wouldn't eat here unless you're staying nearby.

Pub Grub

$$ The Salisbury Arms is a gastropub serving upscale, traditional classics with flair. While they have a bar area and a garden terrace, I'd dine in their elegant restaurant section. The menu ranges from burgers and salads to more sophisticated dishes (book ahead for restaurant, no reservations taken for pub, food served daily 12:00-22:00, across from the pool at 58 Dalkeith Road, +44 131 667 4518, www.thesalisburyarmsedinburgh.co.uk).

$$ The Old Bell Inn, with an old-time sports-bar ambience—fishing, golf, horses, lots of TVs—serves an extensive menu of pub meals with daily specials. This is a classic "snug pub"—all dark woods and brass beer taps, littered with evocative knickknacks (bar tables can be reserved, food served daily until 21:15, 233 Causewayside, +44 131 668 1573, www.oldbelledinburgh.co.uk).

Eateries Around Newington Road

$$ Hanedan serves fresh Turkish food at tiny tables in a cozy dining room. The lamb, fish, and vegetable dishes are all authentic and bursting with flavor, making this a welcome alternative to pub fare (Tue-Sun 12:00-15:00 & 17:30-late, closed Mon, 42 West Preston Street, +44 131 667 4242).

$$ Southpour is a nice place for a local beer, craft cocktail, or reliable meal from a menu of salads, sandwiches, meat dishes, and other comfort foods. The brick walls, wood beams, and giant windows give it a warm and open vibe (don't miss the specials board, Wed-Sun 10:00-22:00, closed Mon-Tue, 1 Newington Road, +44 131 650 1100).

$$ Voujon Restaurant serves a fusion menu of Bengali and Indian cuisines. Vegetarians appreciate the expansive yet inexpensive offerings (daily 17:00-23:00, 107 Newington Road, +44 131 667 5046).

$$$ Apiary has an inviting, casual interior and a hit-or-miss, eclectic menu that mingles various international flavors—they call it "local products with global spices" (two-course lunch deals; Wed-Sun 12:00-14:30 & 17:00-21:00, closed Mon-Tue; 33 Newington Road, +44 131 668 4999).

Groceries: On the main streets near the restaurants you'll find **Sainsbury's Local** and **Co-op** (on South Clerk Street), and **Tesco Express** and another **Sainsbury's Local** one block over on Causewayside (all open late—until at least 22:00).

Memorable Meals Farther Out

$$$$ Rhubarb Restaurant specializes in Old World elegance. It's in "Edinburgh's most handsome house"—an over-the-top riot of antiques, velvet, tassels, and fringe. The plush dark-rhubarb color theme reminds visitors that this was the place where rhubarb was first popularized in Britain. It's a short taxi ride past the other recommended eateries behind Arthur's Seat, in a huge estate with big, shaggy Highland cattle enjoying their salads al fresco. At night, it's a candlelit wonder. Most spend a ton here. Reserve in advance and dress up if you can (daily 12:00-14:00 & 18:00-22:00, afternoon tea served daily 12:00-19:00, in Prestonfield House, Priestfield Road, +44 131 662 2303, www.prestonfield.com).

$$ The Sheep Heid Inn, Edinburgh's oldest and most inviting public house, is equally notable for its history, date-night appeal, and elevated gastropub-type food (with the same owners, and a similar menu, as The Salisbury Arms, above). It's a short cab ride or pleasant 30-minute walk from the B&B neighborhood, but it's worth the effort to dine in this dreamy setting in the presence of past queens and kings—choose between the bar downstairs, dining room upstairs, or outside in the classic garden courtyard. Ask to see—or try—the original skittle alley (a type of bowling game), in a back room. Book ahead before you make the trip (food served Mon-Fri 12:00-21:00, Sat-Sun 12:00-21:30, 43 The Causeway, +44 131 661 7974, www.thesheepheidedinburgh.co.uk).

Edinburgh Connections

BY TRAIN OR BUS

From Edinburgh by Train to: Glasgow (7/hour, 50 minutes), **St. Andrews** (train to Leuchars, 2/hour, 1 hour, then 10-minute bus into St. Andrews), **Stirling** (2/hour, 45 minutes), **Pitlochry** (6/day direct, 2 hours, more with transfer), **Inverness** (6/day direct, 3.5 hours, more with transfer), **Oban** (roughly 6/day, 4.5 hours, change in Glasgow), **York** (3/hour, 2.5 hours), **London** (2/hour, 4.5 hours), **Durham** (2/hour direct, 2 hours, less frequent in winter), **Newcastle** (3/hour, 1.5 hours), **Keswick/Lake District** (8/day to Penrith—more via Carlisle, 1.5 hours, then 40-minute bus ride to Keswick), **Birmingham** (hourly, 5 hours, more with transfer), **Crewe** (every 2 hours, 3 hours), **Bristol,** near Bath (hourly, 6.5 hours), **Blackpool** (about every 2 hours, 3.5 hours, transfer in Preston). Train info: +44 345 748 4950, www.nationalrail.co.uk.

By Citylink Bus: Direct buses go to **Glasgow** (#900, 4/hour, 1.5 hours), **Inverness** (#M90, 8/day, 4 hours), **Pitlochry** (#M90, 8/day, 2.5 hours), and **Stirling** (every 2 hours on #909, 1.5 hours). Bus #913 runs just once each morning to **Glencoe** (4 hours) and **Fort William** (4.5 hours); with a transfer, you can use this bus to reach **Oban** (4.5 hours, change in Tyndrum) and **Portree** on the Isle of Skye (8 hours, change in Fort William). Otherwise, you can reach **Oban, Glencoe, Fort William,** and **Portree** by taking a train to Glasgow, then catching a bus from there. For bus info, stop by the station or call Scottish Citylink (+44 871 266 3333, www.citylink.co.uk); note that Megabus, which shares a parent company, also sells tickets for Citylink buses (www.megabus.com).

Additional long-distance routes may be operated by National Express (www.nationalexpress.com).

BY PLANE

Edinburgh Airport is located eight miles northwest of the center (code: EDI, +44 844 481 8989, www.edinburghairport.com). A **taxi** or **Uber** between the airport and city center costs about £30 (25 minutes to downtown, West End, or Dalkeith Road).

The airport is also well connected to central Edinburgh by tram and bus. Both of these are to the far left as you exit the terminal building: Look for bus stop A; the tram tracks are across the street. **Trams** make several stops in town, including at the West End, along Princes Street, and at St. Andrew Square (£6.50, £9 round-trip, buy ticket from machine, runs every 5-10 minutes from early morning until 23:30, 35 minutes, www.edinburghtrams.com). The Lothian **Airlink bus #100** drops you at Waverley Bridge

(£4.50, £7.50 round-trip, runs every 10 minutes, 30 minutes, +44 131 555 6363, www.lothianbuses.com).

ROUTE TIPS FOR DRIVERS HEADING SOUTH

If you're linking by car to England, note that it's 100 miles south from Edinburgh to Hadrian's Wall; to Durham, it's another 50 miles.

To Hadrian's Wall: From Edinburgh, head south on Dalkeith Road (a handy Cameron Toll Shopping Center with a Sainsbury's grocery and cheap gas is off to your right as you head out of town; gas and parking behind store). Follow Dalkeith Road for about four miles (10 minutes) until you reach the *Sheriffhall* roundabout. Take the exit to A-68 (straight ahead). The A-68 road takes you to Hadrian's Wall in 2.5 hours. You'll pass Jedburgh and its abbey after one hour. (For one last shot of Scotland shopping, there's a bus tour's delight just before Jedburgh, with kilt makers, woolens, and a sheepskin shop.) Across from Jedburgh's lovely abbey is a free parking lot, a good visitors center, and pay WCs. The England/Scotland border is a fun, quick stop (great view, ice cream, and tea caravan). Just after the turn for Colwell, turn right onto the A-6079, and roller-coaster four miles down to Low Brunton. Then turn right onto the B-6318, and stay on it by turning left at Chollerford, following the Roman wall westward.

To Durham: If you're heading straight to Durham, you can take the scenic coastal route on the A-1 (a few more miles than the A-68, but similar time), which takes you near Holy Island and Bamburgh Castle.

PRACTICALITIES

This section covers just the basics on traveling in Scotland (for much more information, see *Rick Steves Scotland*). You'll find free advice on specific topics at RickSteves.com/tips.

MONEY

For currency, Scotland uses the pound sterling (£), also called a "quid": 1 pound (£1) = about $1.30. One pound is broken into 100 pence (p). To convert prices in pounds to dollars, add about 30 percent: £20 = about $26, £50 = about $65. (Check Oanda.com for the latest exchange rates.) While the pound is used throughout the UK, Scotland prints its own bills, which are decorated with Scottish landmarks and VIPs. These are interchangeable with British pound notes, which are widely circulated here.

You'll use your **credit card** for purchases both big (hotels, advance tickets) and small (little shops, food stands). Visa and Mastercard are universal while American Express and Discover are less common. Some European businesses have gone cashless, making a card your only payment option.

A **"tap-to-pay"** or "contactless" card is the most widely accepted and simplest to use: Before departing, check if you have—or can get—a tap-to-pay credit card (look on the card for the symbol—four curvy lines) and consider setting up your smartphone for contactless payment. Let your bank know that you'll be traveling in Europe, adjust your ATM withdrawal limit if needed, and make sure you know the four-digit PIN for each of your cards, both debit and credit (as you may need to use **chip-and-PIN** for certain purchases). Allow time to receive your PIN by mail.

While most transactions are by card these days, **cash** can help you out of a jam if your card randomly doesn't work, and can be useful to pay for tips and local guides. Wait until you arrive to get euros using your **debit card** (airports have plenty of cash machines). European ATMs accept US debit cards with a Visa or Mastercard logo and work just like they do at home—except they spit out local currency instead of dollars. When possible, withdraw cash from a bank-run ATM located just outside that bank (they usually charge lower fees and are more secure).

Whether withdrawing cash at an ATM or paying with a credit card, you'll often be asked whether you want the transaction processed in dollars or in the local currency. To avoid a poor exchange rate, always refuse the conversion and *choose the local currency*.

Although rare, some US cards may not work at self-service payment machines (such as transit-ticket kiosks, tollbooths, or fuel pumps). Usually a tap-to-pay card does the trick in these situations. Carry cash as a backup and look for a cashier who can process your payment if your card is rejected.

Before you leave home, let your bank know when and where you'll be using your credit and debit cards. To keep your cash, cards, and valuables safe when traveling, wear a **money belt**.

STAYING CONNECTED

The simplest solution is to bring your own device—mobile phone, tablet, or laptop—and use it just as you would at home (following the money-saving tips below). For more on phoning, see RickSteves.com/phoning. For a one-hour talk covering tech issues for travelers, see RickSteves.com/mobile-travel-skills. The following instructions apply in Scotland and across Great Britain.

To Call from a US Phone: Phone numbers in this book are presented exactly as you would dial them from a US mobile phone. For international access, press and hold the 0 key until you get a + sign, then dial the country code (44 for Scotland/Great Britain) and phone number (omit the initial zero that's used for domestic calls). To dial from a US landline, replace + with 011 (US/Canada international access code).

From a European Landline: Replace + with 00 (Europe international access code), then dial the country code (44 for Scotland/Great Britain) and phone number (omitting the initial zero).

Within Scotland/Great Britain: To place a domestic call (from a Scottish or British landline or mobile), drop the +44 and dial the phone number (including the initial zero).

Tips: If you bring your mobile phone, consider signing up for an international plan; most providers offer a simple bundle that includes calling, messaging, and data.

Use Wi-Fi whenever possible. Most hotels and many cafés offer free Wi-Fi, and you may also find it at tourist information offices (TIs), major museums, public-transit hubs, and aboard trains and buses. With Wi-Fi you can use your phone or tablet to make free or

Sleep Code

Hotels are classified based on the average price of a standard en suite double room with breakfast in high season.

$$$$	**Splurge:** Most rooms over £180
$$$	**Pricier:** £130-180
$$	**Moderate:** £100-130
$	**Budget:** £60-100
¢	**Backpacker:** Under £60
RS%	**Rick Steves discount**

Unless otherwise noted, credit cards are accepted and free Wi-Fi is available. Comparison-shop by checking prices at several hotels (on each hotel's own website, on a booking site, or by email). For the best deal, *always book directly with the hotel.* Ask for a discount if paying in cash; if the listing includes **RS%,** request a Rick Steves discount.

low-cost domestic and international calls via a calling app such as Skype, WhatsApp, FaceTime, and Google Meet. When you need to get online but can't find Wi-Fi, turn on your cellular network (or turn off airplane mode) just long enough for the task at hand.

Most **hotels** charge a fee for placing calls—ask for rates before you dial. You can use a prepaid international phone card (usually available at newsstands, tobacco shops, and train stations) to call out from your hotel.

SLEEPING

I've categorized my recommended accommodations based on price, indicated with a dollar-sign rating (see sidebar). Book your accommodations as soon as your itinerary is set, especially if you want to stay at one of my top listings or if you'll be traveling during busy times. This is particularly important—especially in smaller towns—because good-quality, good-value, characteristic B&Bs are in short supply—and they book up fast.

Compare prices at several hotels. You can do this by checking hotel websites and booking sites such as Hotels.com or Booking.com. After you've zeroed in on your choice, **book directly with the hotel itself.** This increases the chances that the hotelier will be able to accommodate special needs or requests (such as shifting your reservation). And when you book on the hotel's website, by email, or by phone, the owner avoids the commission paid to booking sites, giving them wiggle room to offer you a discount, a nicer room, or a free breakfast.

For family-run hotels, it's generally best to book your room directly via email or phone. Here's what they'll want to know: number and type of rooms; number of nights; arrival date; departure date; any special requests; and applicable discounts (such as a

Rick Steves discount, cash discount, or promotional rate). Use the European style for writing dates: day/month/year.

An "en suite" room has a bathroom (toilet and shower/tub) attached to the room; a room with a "private bathroom" can mean that the bathroom is all yours, but it's across the hall. If you want your own bathroom inside the room, request "en suite."

Some hotels extend a discount to those who pay cash or stay longer than three nights. And some accommodations offer a special discount for Rick Steves readers, indicated in this guidebook by the abbreviation **"RS%."**

Compared to hotels, bed-and-breakfast places give you double the cultural intimacy for half the price. Personal touches, whether it's joining my hosts for afternoon tea or relaxing by a common fireplace at the end of the day, make staying at a B&B my preferred choice. Many B&Bs take credit cards but may add the card service fee to your bill (about 3 percent). If you'll need to pay cash for your room, plan ahead.

A short-term rental—whether an apartment, house, or room in a private residence—is a popular alternative, especially if you plan to settle in one location for several nights. Websites such as Airbnb, FlipKey, Booking.com, and VRBO let you browse a wide range of properties. Alternatively, rental agencies such as InterhomeUSA.com and RentaVilla.com can provide a more personalized service.

EATING

I've categorized my recommended eateries based on the average price of a typical main course, indicated with a dollar-sign rating (see sidebar).

The traditional fry-up or full Scottish breakfast comes with your choice of eggs, Canadian-style bacon and/or sausage, a grilled tomato, sautéed mushrooms, baked beans, toast and marmalade, and often haggis, black pudding, or a dense potato scone. As an alternative, most hotels serve a healthier continental breakfast as well—with a buffet of yogurt, cereal, fruit, and pastries; and many B&Bs offer vegetarian, organic, gluten-free, or other creative variations on the traditional breakfast.

To dine affordably at classier restaurants, look for "early-bird specials" (sometimes called "pre-theater menus"), which allow you to eat well but early, usually before 18:30 or 19:00 (sometimes on weekdays only).

Smart travelers use pubs (short for "public houses") to eat, drink, get out of the rain, and make new friends. Pub grub is Scotland's best eating value (although not every pub sells food). Pubs that are attached to restaurants are more likely to have fresh, made-to-order food. For about $20, you'll get a basic meal in con-

Restaurant Code

I've assigned each eatery a price category, based on the average cost of a typical main course. Drinks, desserts, and splurge items (steak and seafood) can raise the price considerably.

$$$$ **Splurge:** Most main courses over £20
$$$ **Pricier:** £15-20
$$ **Moderate:** £10-15
$ **Budget:** Under £10

In Scotland, carryout fish-and-chips and other takeout food is **$**, a basic pub or sit-down eatery is **$$**, a gastropub or casual but more upscale restaurant is **$$$**, and a swanky splurge is **$$$$**.

vivial surroundings. The menu is generally hearty and traditional: fish-and-chips, roast beef with Yorkshire pudding, and assorted meat pies, such as steak-and-kidney pie or shepherd's pie (stewed lamb topped with mashed potatoes), with cooked vegetables. But these days, you'll likely find more pasta, curried dishes, and quiche on the menu than traditional fare.

Meals are usually served from 12:00 to 14:00 and from 18:00 to 20:00, not throughout the day. Order drinks and meals at the bar, and pay at the bar (sometimes when you order, sometimes after you eat).

Most pubs have lagers (cold, refreshing, American-style beer), ales (amber-colored, cellar-temperature beer), bitters (hop-flavored ale, perhaps the most typical British beer), and stouts (dark and somewhat bitter, like Guinness).

While bar-hopping tourists generally think in terms of beer, many Scottish pubs are just as enthusiastic about serving whisky. If you are unfamiliar with whisky (what Americans call "Scotch" and the Irish call "whiskey"), it's a great conversation starter. Pubs often have dozens of whiskies available.

Tipping: At pubs and places where you order at the counter, you don't have to tip. At restaurants and fancy pubs with waitstaff, it's standard to tip about 10-12 percent; you can add a bit more for finer dining or extra-good service. Occasionally a service charge is added to your bill, in which case no additional tip is necessary (but check your bill to be sure).

TRANSPORTATION

By Train: Great Britain's train system is one of Europe's best...and most expensive. To see if a rail pass could save you money—as it often does in Britain—check RickSteves.com/rail. If you're buying point-to-point tickets, you'll get the best deals if you book in advance, leave after rush hour (after 9:30 weekdays), or ride the bus. Train reservations are recommended for long journeys or for travel on weekends or holidays (reserve online, at any train station, or by phone). For train schedules or to book, see NationalRail. co.uk. Germany's all-Europe website, Bahn.com, is also a good source for schedules.

By Car: A car is useful for scouring the remote rural sights, but it's an expensive headache in big cities. It's cheaper to arrange most car rentals from the US. For tips on your insurance options, see RickSteves.com/cdw. For navigation, the mapping app on your phone works fine. Bring your driver's license.

Speedy motorways (comparable to our freeways) let you cover long distances in a snap. Remember that the Scottish drive on the left side of the road (and the driver sits on the right side of the car). You'll quickly master Scotland's many roundabouts: Traffic moves clock-wise, cars inside the roundabout have the right-of-way, and entering traffic yields (look to your right as you merge). Note that road-surveillance cameras strictly enforce speed limits by automatically snapping photos of speeders' license plates, then mailing them a ticket.

Be aware of Britain's rules of the road. Ask your car-rental company about them or check the US State Department website (www.travel.state.gov, search for your country in the "Learn About Your Destination" box, then select "Travel and Transportation").

By Bus: Long-distance buses (called "coaches" in Scotland) are about a third slower than trains, but they're also much cheaper—and go many places that trains don't. Most long-haul domestic routes in Scotland are operated by Scottish Citylink (www.citylink.co.uk). Some regional routes are operated by Citylink's Stagecoach service (www.stagecoachbus.com). In peak season, it's worth booking your seat on popular routes at least a few days in advance (at the bus station or TI, on the Citylink website, or by calling +44 0141 352 4444). At slower times, you can just hop on the bus and pay the driver. .

HELPFUL HINTS

Travel Advisories: Before traveling, check updated health and safety conditions, including restrictions for your destination, on the travel pages of the US State Department (www.travel.state. gov) and Centers for Disease Control and Prevention (www.cdc. gov/travel). The US embassy website for Edinburgh is also a good source of information (see below).

Covid Vaccine/Test Requirements: It's possible you'll need to present proof of vaccination against the coronavirus and/or a negative Covid-19 test result to board a plane to Europe or back to the US. Carefully check requirements for each country you'll visit well before you depart, and again a few days before your trip. See the websites listed above for current requirements.

Emergency and Medical Help: For any emergency service—ambulance, police, or fire—call **112 or 999** from a mobile phone or landline. If you get sick, do as the Scots do and go to a pharmacist for advice. Or ask at your hotel for help—they'll know the nearest medical and emergency services.

For **passport problems,** call the **US Consulate in Edinburgh** (+44 131 556 8315, no walk-in passport services, https://uk.usembassy.gov/embassy-consulates/edinburgh) or the **Canadian Consulate in Edinburgh** (+44 1250 870 831 during business hours, www.unitedkingdom.gc.ca).

Theft or Loss: To replace a passport, you'll need to go in person to an embassy or consulate (see above). Cancel and replace your credit and debit cards by calling these 24-hour US numbers: Visa (dial +1 303 967 1096), Mastercard (dial +1 636 722 7111), and American Express (dial +1 336 393 1111). From a landline, you can call these US numbers collect by going through a local operator.

File a police report either on the spot or within a day or two; you'll need it to submit an insurance claim for lost or stolen items, and it can help with replacing your passport or credit and debit cards. For more information, see RickSteves.com/help.

Time: Scotland uses the 24-hour clock. It's the same through 12:00 noon, then keep going: 13:00, 14:00, and so on. Scotland, like the rest of Great Britain, is five/eight hours ahead of the East/West Coasts of the US (and one hour earlier than most of continental Europe).

Business Hours: Most stores are open Monday through Saturday (roughly 9:00 or 10:00 to 17:00 or 18:00). In cities, some stores stay open later on Wednesday or Thursday (until 19:00 or 20:00). On Sundays sightseeing attractions are generally open, many street markets are lively with shoppers, banks and many shops are closed, and public transportation options are fewer (for example, no bus service to or from smaller towns).

Sightseeing: Many popular sights come with long lines—not to get in, but to buy a ticket. Visitors who buy tickets online in advance (or who have a museum pass covering these key sights) can skip the line and waltz right in. Advance tickets are generally timed-entry, meaning you're guaranteed admission on a certain date and time.

For some sights, buying ahead is required (tickets aren't sold at the sight and it's the only way to get in). At other sights, buying ahead is recommended to skip the line and save time. And for many sights, advance tickets are available but unnecessary: At these uncrowded sights you can simply arrive, buy a ticket, and go in.

Use my advice in this book as a guide. Note any must-see sights that sell out long in advance and be prepared to buy tickets early. If you do your research, you'll know the smart strategy.

PRACTICALITIES

Given how precious your vacation time is, I'd book in advance both where it's required (as soon as your dates are firm) and where it will save time in a long line (in some cases, you can do this even on the day you plan to visit).

Holidays and Festivals: Great Britain celebrates many holidays, which can close sights and attract crowds (book hotel rooms ahead). For information on holidays and festivals, check Scotland's tourism website, VisitScotland.com. For a simple list showing major—though not all—events, see RickSteves.com/festivals.

Numbers and Stumblers: What Americans call the second floor of a building is the first floor in Europe. Europeans write dates as day/month/year, so Christmas 2024 is 25/12/24. For most measurements, Great Britain uses the metric system: A kilogram is 2.2 pounds, and a liter is about a quart. For driving distances, they use miles.

RESOURCES FROM RICK STEVES

This Snapshot guide is excerpted from my latest edition of *Rick Steves Scotland*, one of many titles in my ever-expanding series of guidebooks on European travel. I also produce a public television series, *Rick Steves' Europe*, and a public radio show, *Travel with Rick Steves*. My free online video library, Rick Steves Classroom Europe, offers a searchable database of short video clips on European history, culture, and geography (Classroom.RickSteves.com). My website, RickSteves.com, offers free travel information, a forum for travelers' comments, guidebook updates, my travel blog, an online travel store, and information on European rail passes and our tours of Europe. If you're bringing a mobile device, you can download my free Rick Steves Audio Europe app, featuring dozens of self-guided audio tours of the top sights in Europe, including the Edinburgh Royal Mile Walk audio tour, and travel interviews about Scotland. For more information, see RickSteves.com/audioeurope. You can also follow me on Facebook, Twitter, and Instagram.

ADDITIONAL RESOURCES

Tourist Information: www.visitscotland.com
Passports and Red Tape: www.travel.state.gov
Packing List: www.ricksteves.com/packing
Travel Insurance: www.ricksteves.com/insurance
Cheap Flights: www.kayak.com or www.google.com/flights
Airplane Carry-on Restrictions: www.tsa.gov
Updates for This Book: www.ricksteves.com/update

HOW WAS YOUR TRIP?

To share your tips, concerns, and discoveries after using this book, please fill out the survey at RickSteves.com/feedback. Thanks in advance—it helps a lot.

PRACTICALITIES

INDEX

Explore Europe

At ricksteves.com you can browse through thousands of articles, videos, photos and radio interviews, plus find a wealth of money-saving travel tips for planning your dream trip. And with our mobile-friendly website, you can easily access all this great travel information anywhere you go.

TV Shows

Preview the places you'll visit by watching entire half-hour episodes of *Rick Steves' Europe* (choose from all 100 shows) on-demand, for free.

ricksteves.com

your travel dreams into affordable reality

Radio Interviews

Enjoy ready access to Rick's vast library of radio interviews covering travel tips and cultural insights that relate specifically to your Europe travel plans.

Travel Forums

Learn, ask, share! Our online community of savvy travelers is a great resource for first-time travelers to Europe, as well as seasoned pros.

Travel News

Subscribe to our free Travel News e-newsletter, and get monthly updates from Rick on what's happening in Europe.

Classroom Europe®

Check out our free resource for educators with 500 short video clips from the *Rick Steves' Europe* TV show.

Audio Europe™

Pack Light and Right

Gear up for your next adventure at ricksteves.com

Light Luggage

Pack light and right with Rick Steves' affordable, custom-designed rolling carry-on bags, backpacks, day packs and shoulder bags.

Accessories

From packing cubes to moneybelts and beyond, Rick has personally selected the travel goodies that will help your trip go smoother.

Rick Steves has

Save time and energy

This guidebook is your independent-travel toolkit. But for all it delivers, it's still up to you to devote the time and energy it takes to manage the preparation and logistics that are essential for a happy trip. If that's a hassle, there's a solution.

Rick Steves Tours

A Rick Steves tour takes you to Europe's most interesting places with great

with minimum stress

guides and small groups. We follow Rick's favorite itineraries, ride in comfy buses, stay in family-run hotels, and bring you intimately close to the Europe you've traveled so far to see. Most importantly, we take away the logistical headaches so you can focus on the fun.

Join the fun

This year we'll take thousands of free-spirited travelers—nearly half of them repeat customers—along with us on 50 different itineraries, from Athens to Istanbul. Is a Rick Steves tour the right fit for your travel dreams?

Find out at ricksteves.com, where you can also check seat availability and sign up. Europe is best experienced with happy travel partners. We hope you can join us.

See our itineraries at ricksteves.com

A Guide for Every Trip

BEST OF GUIDES

Full-color guides in an easy-to-scan format. Focused on top sights and experiences in the most popular European destinations

Best of England
Best of Europe
Best of France
Best of Germany
Best of Ireland
Best of Italy
Best of Scotland
Best of Spain

COMPREHENSIVE GUIDES

City, country, and regional guides printed on Bible-thin paper. Packed with detailed coverage for a multi-week trip exploring iconic sights and venturing off the beaten path

Amsterdam & the Netherlands
Barcelona
Belgium: Bruges, Brussels, Antwerp & Ghent
Berlin
Budapest
Croatia & Slovenia
Eastern Europe
England
Florence & Tuscany
France
Germany
Great Britain
Greece: Athens & the Peloponnese
Iceland
Ireland
Istanbul
Italy
London
Paris
Portugal
Prague & the Czech Republic
Provence & the French Riviera
Rome
Scandinavia
Scotland
Sicily
Spain
Switzerland
Venice
Vienna, Salzburg & Tirol

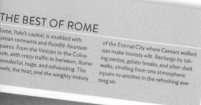

THE BEST OF ROME

Rome, Italy's capital, is studded with Roman remnants and floodlit-fountain squares. From the Vatican to the Colosseum, with crazy traffic in between, Rome is wonderful, huge, and exhausting. The crowds, the heat, and the weighty history of the Eternal City where Caesars walked can make tourists wilt. Recharge by taking siestas, gelato breaks, and after-dark walks, strolling from one atmospheric square to another in the refreshing evening air.

...ired **Pantheon**—which ...rgest dome until the ...early 2,000 years old ...day over 1,500).

...ol of Athens in the Vat-
...bodies the humanistic
...ance.

...s, gladiators fought
...e another, entertaining
...00.

...this Rome *please...*

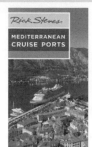

POCKET GUIDES
Compact color guides for shorter trips

Amsterdam	Paris
Athens	Prague
Barcelona	Rome
Florence	Venice
Italy's Cinque Terre	Vienna
London	
Munich & Salzburg	

SNAPSHOT GUIDES
Focused single-destination coverage

Basque Country: Spain & France
Copenhagen & the Best of Denmark
Dublin
Dubrovnik
Edinburgh
Hill Towns of Central Italy
Krakow, Warsaw & Gdansk
Lisbon
Loire Valley
Madrid & Toledo
Milan & the Italian Lakes District
Naples & the Amalfi Coast
Nice & the French Riviera
Normandy
Northern Ireland
Norway
Reykjavík
Rothenburg & the Rhine
Sevilla, Granada & Southern Spain
St. Petersburg, Helsinki & Tallinn
Stockholm

CRUISE PORTS GUIDES
Reference for cruise ports of call

Mediterranean Cruise Ports
Scandinavian & Northern European
  Cruise Ports

Complete your library with...

TRAVEL SKILLS & CULTURE
*Study up on travel skills and gain
insight on history and culture*

Europe 101
Europe Through the Back Door
Europe's Top 100 Masterpieces
European Christmas
European Easter
European Festivals
For the Love of Europe
Italy for Food Lovers
Travel as a Political Act

PHRASE BOOKS & DICTIONARIES
French
French, Italian & German
German
Italian
Portuguese
Spanish

PLANNING MAPS
Britain, Ireland & London
Europe
France & Paris
Germany, Austria & Switzerland
Iceland
Ireland
Italy
Scotland
Spain & Portugal

Photo Credits

Avalon Travel
Hachette Book Group
1700 Fourth Street
Berkeley, CA 94710

Printed in Canada by Friesens.
Fourth Edition. First printing February 2023.

ISBN 978-1-64171-533-1

For the latest on Rick's talks, guidebooks, tours, public television series, and public radio show, contact Rick Steves' Europe, 130 Fourth Avenue North, Edmonds, WA 98020, +1 425 771 8303, RickSteves.com, rick@ricksteves.com.

Rick Steves' Europe

Managing Editor: Jennifer Madison Davis
Assistant Managing Editor: Cathy Lu
Editors: Glenn Eriksen, Suzanne Kotz, Rosie Leutzinger, Teresa Nemeth, Jessica Shaw, Carrie Shepherd
Editorial & Production Assistant: Megan Simms
Researcher: Cameron Hewitt
Contributor: Gene Openshaw
Graphic Content Director: Sandra Hundacker
Maps & Graphics: Orin Dubrow, David C. Hoerlein, Lauren Mills, Mary Rostad, Laura Terrenzio

Avalon Travel

Senior Editor and Series Manager: Maddy McPrasher
Editors: Jamie Andrade, Rachael Sablik
Proofreader: Patrick Collins
Indexer: Stephen Callahan
Production & Typesetting: Christine DeLorenzo, Lisi Baldwin, Rue Flaherty
Cover Design: Kimberly Glyder Design
Maps & Graphics: Kat Bennett, Lohnes & Wright

Although every effort was made to ensure that the information was correct at the time of going to press, the author and publisher do not assume and hereby disclaim any liability to any party for any loss or damage caused by errors, omissions, kilt malfunction, or any potential travel disruption due to labor or financial difficulty, whether such errors or omissions result from negligence, accident, or any other cause.

Let's Keep on Travelin'

Your trip doesn't need to end.

Follow Rick on social media!